There's a Bee
In My Begonias

There's a Bee In My Begonias

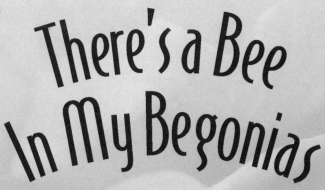

Garden Paths and Prayers

BERNADETTE McCARVER SNYDER

Liguori
LIGUORI, MISSOURI

Published by Liguori Publications
Liguori, Missouri
www.liguori.org
www.catholicbooksonline.com

Library of Congress Cataloging-in-Publication Data

Snyder, Bernadette McCarver.
    There's a bee in my begonias : garden paths and prayers / Bernadette McCarver Snyder.
        p. cm.
    ISBN 0-7648-0787-0 (pbk.)
    1. Gardeners—Prayer-books and devotions—English. 2. Gardens—Religious aspects
Christianity—Meditations. I. Title: There is a bee in my begonias. II. Title.

BV4596.G36 S69 2002
242—dc21   2001038135

Printed in the United States of America
05 04 03 02 01   5 4 3 2 1
First edition

I dedicate this book to all my "dirty hands" friends—those who delight with me in digging for and discovering the glories of God's garden surprises. Flowers must depend on friends—sun, rain, breeze, butterflies and bees—for nourishment, food, and regular visits. I, too, depend on friends for the nourishment of exchanged ideas, shared food, and fun. They have added so much pleasure to my everyday journey and my spiritual journey—and I am grateful to each and every one. You know who you are.

The kiss of the sun for pardon,
The song of the birds for mirth—
One is nearer God's heart in a garden
Than anywhere else on earth.

✳️ *Contents* ✳️

Introduction

January and February

Happy Apple New Year 3
Bloomin' Belladonna 4
The "Clean Hands" Garden 6
Are You a Hopper or a Waddler? 7
The Knight's Unforgettable Story 8
Focus on the Crocus 10
Dew Drop In! 11
The Hardy Head-Start Runner 12

March

Spring Is Springing—Whoopity-Do! 15
The Sultan's Turban 16
A Purple Olive? 17
Heart's-Ease 18
A Breezy Blossom 19
There's a Lion on My Lawn 20
Mirror, Mirror On the Wall... 21
Cardiac Arrest 22
Livin' in Clover 23
I Can't Believe It's Not Butter! 24

April

Myrtle and Murtle 27
Good Morning to You! 28
The Dandelion Corsage 29

Poached Eggs and Baby-Blues 30
The Gold Rush 31
Herb Who? 32
Hello, Funny Face 33
Wistfully Misspelled 34
Barbara's Buttons, Queen Anne's Lace, Black-Eyed Susan 35
Parslied Petunias? 36
A Grass Bouquet 38

May

A Rose Is a Rose Is a Strawberry? 41
The King's Flower 42
You Are My Sunshine 43
The Teary-Eyed Fritillary 44
The Old Man's Beard 45
How Could You Forget? 46
Sweet Surprise 47
Granny's Bonnet 48
Lend an Ear 49
At Your Service 50

June

Love Me, Love Me Not 53
Dahling, It's a Dahlia! 54
Don't Needle the Pincushion 55
Up, Up, and Away… 56
Into the Valley Again 57
Busy Lizzie 58
Make a Wish 59
All That Jazz 60
The "Mission" of Botanists 61
Sweet William Who? 62

CONTENTS

July

Moonstones and Blue Diamonds 65
The Old/New Flower 66
The Foxy One 67
Miss Muffet, Beware 68
Whose Nose Is Out of Joint? 69
Purple Earrings 71
The Milky Way 72
Creamcups and Marshmallows 73
Obedient Dragons 74
The Sunbather 75
Let a Smile Be Your Umbrella 76

August

Achoo…God Bless You 79
The Begonia and the Botanist 80
What Time Is It? 81
Pop Art 82
Smile! 83
Catching Some ZZZs 84
Mexican Hats and Hedgehogs 85
The Dark of Night 86
Yucky or Not? 87
Plants to Dye For! 88

September

Is There a Doctor in the House? 91
What's in a Name? 92
Mum's the Word 93
Psst!…Pass It On… 94
The Garden Wall 95

The Dinosaur's Garden 96
Honestly Now! 97
The Wedding Gift 98
Fashionably Late Flowers 100

October

It's a Flact! 103
Anyone for Tea? 104
Getting Squashed! 105
A Gawky Yard Bird 106
Sooo Soft 107
A Windy Story 108
Boo! A Ghost! 109
The Friendly Witch 110

November & December

The Ivy League 113
The December Decorator 114
Deck the Halls 115
Gold and What? 116
Star Light, Star Bright 118
The Ambassador 119

Appendix

Garden Tips and Quips 125

✎ Introduction ✎

Oh, Adam was a gardener
And God, who made him, sees
That half a gardener's work
Is done upon his knees.

RUDYARD KIPLING

Ah yes, gardens—like a few other things in my life—have often brought me to my knees. What about you? Do you like to dig in the dirt, to plant, to putter? Or do you prefer to walk in the woods or stroll through a park—and be surprised by the glory of God's beauties planted hither and yon? Whichever type of "gardening" you choose, the sight of a garden in full bloom can really bring you to your knees.

In my own tiny little patio patch of plants, I have a small sign that reads, "Gardeners know the best dirt." And I do indeed know about dirt. Even when I wear gloves to garden, I end up with dirt under my fingernails, on my face, in my shoes, and all over my knees. Maybe that's why I felt inspired to "dig up some dirt" for this book about the little-known secrets behind flower names and the fun facts you can find in flower family trees—and then to mix in some of my own homegrown prayers.

I've noticed that hands-on gardeners are often like a bee in the begonias or a praying mantis in the petunias. We're always buzzing from flower to flower or rubbing our hands together to complain to God about too many bugs, too little water, too many weeds, too little time. But when you plant a packet of seeds and watch those tiny little nothings turn into a bouquet of beautiful somethings, you

know it's time to rub your hands together with delight and prayers of thanksgiving.

You learn that a garden needs good soil, water, light—and sometimes a fence! For a happy life, you need the same. You need a little fence to get some private quiet time, but you also need occasional showers of friendship and that Light from above. As for soil, you probably know that another word for good soil is *humus,* which comes from the Latin word meaning "humility." And it doesn't take long to get that—whether you're digging in a garden or walking through one. Oh, and you may have noticed that if you substitute "U" for "I," the word "soil" becomes "soul"!

Well, enough of that. Come join me as we wander through the garden, through the year. Let's do some digging—and some praying—together.

A wise person once said that God must have left the sky like an empty canvas where we could each paint our own pictures, dream our own dreams. Although this is a book about flowers, it does not include illustrations of each flower so you can paint your own memories of gardens past or dream of tomorrow's bouquets.

There's a Bee In My Begonias

January & February

*The most noteworthy thing about gardeners
is that they are always optimistic,
always enterprising, and never satisfied.
They always look forward to doing better
than they have ever done before.*

VITA SACKVILLE-WEST

Happy Apple New Year!

Y ou may have tried the Christmas custom of serving wassail (or spiced apple juice or cider) as a toast to "good health," and you've probably sung the Christmas song about going a-wassailing, but did you know this was once an old January custom? And a strange one at that!

After dark, farmworkers and their families would carry horns and a pail of cider out into the orchard. They would pour the cider around the roots of an apple tree and place a piece of toast soaked in cider into the tree's branches. Then they would blow the horns and sing a wassailing song to the tree, wishing it good health and a good crop in the coming year.

Well, there's an apple tree in my backyard, but if I went out there after dark on a cold January night and started blowing a horn and singing a song, my neighbors might call the wassailing police.

I do love old traditions and I am sorely tempted to try this one but even without being wassailed, my apple tree has always burst forth with clouds of white blossoms every spring so maybe I better leave well enough alone.

Lord, I'm often tempted to try something new or something old that's new to me. You may have noticed that I've tried that with prayer too. I went on that retreat where we danced around a bonfire on a cold winter night and blew smoking incense into one another's faces. The incense gave me a coughing fit and while the others meditated, all I could think of was how my feet were freezing.

Although the bonfire and incense didn't work for me, you know and I know, Lord, that I'll probably keep trying new things. But for right now, I really enjoy our little daily prayer chats. So I hope you won't mind if I don't try wassailing you or the apple tree.

Bloomin' Belladonna

When "the weather outside is frightful" and the Christmas decorations have been stored away and there are no garden flowers in the backyard to bring in and brighten up the place, you can still have a blooming good time—with belladonna! This is the kind of Christmas "leftover" you want to have around in January.

Every Christmas, a friend gives me a gift that is not gift-wrapped. It's a green plastic pot, filled with dirt that has a big round brown ugly thing sticking up in the middle of it. Sound beautiful? It isn't—but it is. It's the bulb of an amaryllis—also known as a Belladonna Lily—ready to be "forced" into bloom for my January enjoyment.

And it is enjoyment! All I have to do is water it well and put it in a sunny spot by my patio door. Almost instantly, green shoots begin to sprout from the big round brown ugly thing and they shoot up as fast as a growing teenager. Every morning, they're taller than the day before!

Next comes a bud that I watch get fatter every day. Then one morning, my sleepy eyes open wide when I see the bud has blossomed into a whole clu e r of big bright trumpet-shaped flowers that are waving and trumpeting "good morning" to me. What a happy January surprise!

You might know that the word *belladonna* translates to "beautiful lady," and this flower is truly a beauty to behold—a garden glory in the dead of winter.

Lord, before I found out the amaryllis was also known as a bella-donna, I had only heard of the poisonous belladonna plant, which is a member of the "deadly nightshade" family. Now I've learned that the bulb of the amaryllis is also poisonous. This has taught me two lessons.

Something good and beautiful can grow from an ugly and even poi-sonous beginning. And I should never judge people—or plants—by their relatives or their beginnings.

Thank you, Lord, for so many good and happy families, and please bless and protect those who are not lucky enough to have been born into such a family. Thanks, too, Lord, for a beautiful lesson from the beautiful amaryllis!

The "Clean Hands" Garden

January welcomes a new year, new resolutions, and a mailbox full of flower catalogs. In the midst of cold and snow, I hold in my clean hands, bouquets of perfectly petaled flowers in every color of the rainbow. With no sign of shovel, weeder, fertilizer, or trowel in my family room, my non-calloused fingers thumb through pages of gardens fit for a king, laid out by a horticulturist and tended by full-time gardeners. I sigh, I yearn, I wish. But unless I find an old lamp with a genie in it, I know that my garden will not even vaguely resemble any of those pictures.

And yet, hope springs eternal. Every year, I start planning and plotting. I plan which plot I can dig up when and I plot which plants I can try this year that I never planned before. Shall I try lobelia or astilbe, cow parsley or cotton grass, ragwort or buckthorn? Yes, yes, I know. I'll probably plant most of the same things I do every year—petunias and pansies, begonias and geraniums—because I love them so. But I will also try something new that catches my eye and it may hate my garden and wither away in a few weeks—or it may just love where it has been planted and settle down to be my new best friend. That's all part of the mystery and the fun of a garden.

Well, Lord, as you can see, I've spent way too much time turning catalog pages instead of turning over a new leaf for the new year. I should have been making resolutions and setting spiritual goals as well as garden goals. I should have been telling you how great thou art to have thought up all these strange and exotic and colorful and beautiful growing things. I should have been praising you for planting them on my planet. What great gifts you've given your sometimes ungrateful child. Thanks, Lord. I love ya.

Are You a Hopper or a Waddler?

In the early months of the year, my part of the world is often covered with snow and ice. It's easy to assume that under the white coverlet, life is on hold—nothing is growing or moving. Wrong! I recently heard about a group who went on a wintry nature walk and the leader of the group told them to be on the lookout for tracks. She said, "The landscape may seem still and barren but there is a lot of wildlife out there on the move. You might find several types of tracks—hoppers, bounders, walkers, or waddlers!" They soon found hopping rabbit tracks, bounding deer tracks, and one possible walking bear track—but the waddling tracks probably belonged to some of the hikers! The guide might have suggested they also look for signs of wildflowers. Even in a snowy field, there are plant survivors searching for a tiny crevice to peek out and greet the world. Seeds and bulbs are lying in wait, gathering strength to burst forth in full glory, turning the stark forest into a wild garden of glories. No matter how bleak the landscape, the busy world of plants is just in swaddling clothes, waiting to hop, bound, walk, or waddle into our lives again.

Lord, sometimes my landscape seems bleak—and not just in snowy weather. I feel lifeless, smothered, buried, under a blanket of cold responsibilities and frozen dreams. My spirits sag, my faith flags, and I yearn for the warm spring rains of hope, the summer sunshine of joy. But don't worry, Lord. I'll get over it.

I know it will happen. It has before. I'll find a crevice to peek out. I'll start to waddle, then walk, and finally hop and bound back into your arms. Thanks, Lord, for always being patient. Thanks for always helping my icicles melt.

The Knight's Unforgettable Story

Even though today's world is computerized, downsized, oh-so-modernized and sometimes dehumanized, most people still get a bit sentimental about Valentine's Day—and that calls for flowers, either fresh blossoms or flowery verses. Bouquets appear on executives' desks and on kitchen tables and are pictured on expensive greeting cards and on crayoned notes made by hand with construction paper.

In addition to red hearts and red roses, the flower that most often appears on Valentine cards (as part of the design *and* the message) is the forget-me-not—although the flower itself won't bloom until much later. But why was this little blue flower given that name?

Well, according to a sad but romantic legend, a German knight once picked a bouquet of blue flowers for his beloved as they walked along a riverbank. As he turned to give her the bouquet, his foot slipped, he fell into the river, and just before he drowned, he threw the flowers to her and shouted, "Forget me not." And that tragic tale led to this old Valentine verse:

> *The Lady Fair of the Knight so true*
> *Remembered his helpless lot,*
> *And she cherished the flowers of brightest hue*
> *And braided her hair with the blossoms blue*
> *And called them Forget-Me-Not.*

The story is sad but it gave this little blue flower a name that no one can forget!

Lord, Lord, what a time of year this is—watching for a groundhog to stick his nose out and predict the weather and enjoying gifts of hothouse bouquets and flowery phrases. We gardeners are always watching the weather, too, wondering when to weed, feed, or seed. And in cold February, we are already looking forward to our own homegrown bouquets and the flowery compliments we just might get as a reward for our carefully tended patches of earth. Thanks, Lord, for such warm thoughts on such cold days.

Focus on the Crocus

Every year, a magical thing happens in my front yard. It's almost like "Hocus-pocus, tadah!…a *crocus*!"

It will be a wintry, shivery morning, with no hint of spring in the air, when I go out to the mailbox, and what to my wondering eyes should appear but some little green shoots and a purple, yellow, or white flower smiling up at me. Although I planted a few crocus bulbs around my light post several years ago, I always forget that until… tadah!…the crocus shows up like magic when I least expect it—and when I most need it.

Actually, the crocus is a good lesson for us all. It's so tiny we could pass it by without even a howdy-do. It doesn't make a big splash to attract our attention. It just shows up like a colorful messenger, telling us other blossoms will soon awake, promising us another springtime feast of flowers.

But the quiet crocus has another magical surprise: it belongs to a family that is worth millions of dollars! A very expensive spice called saffron comes from a tiny crocus flower—and sometimes, measured ounce for ounce, saffron sells for more than gold! It takes four thousand crocus stigma (those little golden pollen-carrying center parts) to make *one ounce* of saffron so maybe that's why it's so valuable.

But wait! There's even more to the crocus family story. Not only is it rich, it has a spiritual side too! In the Middle Ages, monks sometimes used that saffron "gold" instead of real gold leaf to make those beautiful "illuminated" pages of spiritual books.

Lord, help me to focus on the crocus today. Remind me that those who seem small and insignificant can be valuable, and those who are rich can be spiritual! Thank you for all the "messengers" you send, offering hope and beauty and faith in the future. Thank you for all the magic in every day. What fun to have your hocus-pocus surprises!

Dew Drop In!

I t's about time now for the snowdrops to drop in and say howdy. And a welcome visit it is! Although in some areas, they bloom as early as January, they are sometimes called "Fair maids of February," and those pretty droopy little white blossoms often appear even later in my garden. Because of their bright snow-white blossoms, bunches of snowdrops were once gathered as soon as they bloomed and displayed in the house to symbolically "cleanse" the home after the drab days of winter.

In contrast to these tiny blooms, there is also a beautiful shrub known as a Snowdrop Tree. Because it has white flowers hanging upside down like tasseled bells along the underside of its branches, it's also called Silver Bell. The tree's botanical name is "halesia." It's named for Stephen Hales who helped lay out England's botanical gardens at Kew and designed the flues for the "Great Stove" greenhouse there. Hales made many *big* botanical discoveries but was said to be just as happy with his little discovery that you can put a small teacup upside down in the bottom of a pie and that will keep the juices from overflowing the pan! Now that's my kind of a guy—a gardener who can also cook!

Dear Lord, I do wander on, don't I—from a flower to a tree to a pie! I'm sure you've noticed how I get behind schedule most days because I keep wandering off the path to investigate something that catches my eye beyond the horizon or over the rainbow. But it's your fault, you know. You created all these marvels in my world and gave me the taste for trivia and the urge to discover. My life would have been much simpler if you had designed me to stick to the straight-and-narrow road— but I'm glad you didn't, since it's lots more fun to wander down the road less traveled!

The Hardy Head-Start Runner

Long before other spring bloomers arrive in my garden, the forsythia has gotten a head start! One day it seems like there is nothing there but a bunch of dead stalks and the next time I pass by, I notice something new—the branches are suddenly full of tightly rolled buds, just waiting for a bit of sunshine to pop out and surprise me. The forsythia can't wait—and I can't either—so I cut a few branches and put them in some warm water and the forsythia happily blooms in my house before it blooms in the yard.

The first time I did that, when the blossoms died and I started to throw out the branches, I saw there were roots on them so I planted them—and by the end of summer, I had a second forsythia bush. Now I have three large forsythias in different parts of the yard and every spring, they try to outdo one another, seeing which one can bloom the brightest, the earliest and the longest.

The forsythia reaches across the fence and waves to neighbors and startles passersby by making my yard look like sunshine even on the gloomiest day. So if you don't have a forsythia bush, get one right away. You don't have to water it or feed it or do anything for it. You can trim it way back and it doesn't mind. Once it makes itself at home in your yard, it takes care of itself and you have a friend forever.

Sometimes I feel guilty, Lord, for not ever doing as much for the forsythia as I do for so many others in my garden family. But I do talk to it frequently and tell it how beautiful it is and how much I appreciate it. Some of my plant—and people—friends expect (and probably deserve) more regular attention. But the longtime ones are like the forsythia—no matter what, friends forever. I sometimes get busy and neglect you too, Lord. I'm glad you're like the forsythia.

March

*The beauties of nature
for me must be one of the joys of heaven.*

JANE AUSTEN

Spring Is Springing... Whoopity-Do!

In Wales, March 1 is celebrated as Saint David's Day and people wear leeks or daffodils in their buttonholes to celebrate. And, according to an old gardening book, in a place called Lanarkshire, March 1 is called "Whoopity Scoorie Day," and bells are rung to chase winter away.

Well, I'm for all that—daffodils and whoopity and chasing winter away. The coming of spring is always cause for celebration and I identify with the daffy-dill since I am usually stricken with spring fever and act even daffier than usual. However, daffodils don't usually bloom in my yard as early as March 1 so should I go to the grocer's and search for a leek to wear—or would that be too daffy? Maybe I better just celebrate with some potato/leek soup for dinner.

We gardeners are not the only ones who celebrate those bright cheery yellow daffodils. Poets, writers, and artists are drawn to them too. Dorothy Wordsworth described daffodils that "tossed and reeled and danced, and seemed as if they verily laughed with the wind...." Her famous brother, William, immortalized them with, "I wandered lonely as a cloud...when all at once I saw a crowd, a host of golden daffodils."

Well, Lord, spring is springing and my daffodils will soon be dancing, but I am reminded that another name for the daffodil is the Lent Lily. It's that time again so I guess I'll have to quell the whoopity for a bit. Although no one welcomes the idea of Lent and repent, it really is a blessing to have this quiet time to pray and to ponder. It isn't a time to be sad. I can rejoice as well as repent—rejoice in the new life just beginning in my garden and use that example as encouragement for me to seek new growth in my spiritual life. And if I do enough weeding and seeding, by Easter I will burst forth with a great whoopity of alleluias!

The Sultan's Turban

As the March winds blow and I look out my front window to watch the bright cheery tulips nodding their heads to and fro, I seldom think of Suleiman the Magnificent, Sultan of Turkey. But I should. You know why? Well, according to a tulip tale, there was once an ambassador to this Sultan's court who was surprised to see that men there wore colorful flowers tucked inside their turbans. The ambassador had never seen that type of flower before so he took some of the flower bulbs home when he returned to Europe.

The sultan's flowers flourished there but they were "flying under false colors." You see, the ambassador thought the flowers—like the hats—were called "turbans" so he gave them the Latinized name for the Arabic word for turban. And the name "tulip" took root!

Since they were used as hat decorations, these bright beauties probably grew wild in the fields of Turkey, but in 1634–1637, in Holland and surrounding countries, a wild speculative binge took place that was called "tulipomania." During this period, tulip bulbs sold for large amounts of money and tulip speculation was rampant! Today tulip bulbs are affordable and blossom in many parts of the world—including my small part. So I am grateful to that ambassador—even if he was a mis-namer.

I am often guilty of being a mis-namer too. I meet someone new and, in my head, give her the name Ugly. After I get to know her, I realize I should have given her the name Delightful, Loving, or Generous. Sometimes I am given a new job to do and I give it the name Don't Wanna. Once I get going on the job, I realize I should have called it Opportunity, Steppingstone, or Ain't I Lucky!

Thanks, Lord, for forgiving my Hate-at-First-Sights and for teaching me to look and learn before labeling.

A Purple Olive?

The lilac is an elegantly old-fashioned favorite that grew in my grandma's yard and now grows in mine. Its luscious grape-like clusters of pale purple flowers have a hauntingly beautiful fragrance. The lilac is related to the privet that makes great hedges but has white flowers with an aroma that most people find hauntingly "unpleasant," to be polite. And would you believe—both the lilac and the privet are distant cousins of the olive family!

It seems that, once they are established, lilacs—like olives—live on and on. Early settlers often planted lilacs by a front porch and years after the settlers had moved on, the lilacs still bloomed. And even when a lilac dies, if the wood is burned, the smoke is filled with that hauntingly beautiful sweet lilac perfume.

Thinking of all this and remembering my grandma's wonderful lilacs in full bloom, I carefully planted a lilac in what I considered a perfect spot and tended it devotedly. It never bloomed. I moved it. Still no blooms. Finally, when we were redoing the patio and the lilac was in the way, I quickly dumped it in a hole right next to the garage where it would inhale gasoline fumes. And it has been blooming and perfuming ever since. But so far, no olives.

Lord, I guess the lilac must also be a distant cousin of humans. Sometimes you can tend them carefully and they refuse to bloom. Other times, they can be planted in the worst spot and they thrive and blossom for the rest of their lives. Maybe this is as puzzling to you as it is to the rest of us, Lord, but I know you love us all, no matter how puzzling we might be. And that's a hauntingly beautiful thing to remember.

Heart's-Ease

For some reason, the shy little purple violet has always seemed a romantic flower to me—and my idea of the most romantic bouquet would be a bunch of purple violets, centered with one pink rose, and circled with green leaves. Maybe I think it's romantic because the violet leaf is heart-shaped and another name for the violet is heart's-ease, or maybe I once read a novel where the hero sent the heroine such a bouquet. I just don't know why but I do know that if I ever receive a bouquet like that, it will give me heart's ease—or maybe a heart attack caused by such a big surprise!

Since I long ago gave up on getting the bouquet, I determined I would at least have violets growing in my yard. I planted some, spoke sweetly to them, and each spring the violets returned and shyly bloomed on their tiny short stems. As soon as I spotted the first ones, I would pick a petite bouquet—with the heart-shaped leaves of course—for my kitchen window sill.

Then one summer we decided to have an "analyst" come and advise us about improving our lawn. He walked all around, looking very official, filled out a long form and noted his recommendations. He listed all the "weeds" we needed to get rid of—and one of them was the violet! Weed indeed! I knew immediately the analyst was an insensitive, unfeeling clod and told him to begone. That summer, our lawn didn't improve but I kept my violets!

Can you imagine that, Lord—a "professional" thinking one of your loveliest flowers is a weed! Sad to say, I guess there are those who think some of your loveliest people are weeds too. Well, there's just no explaining some improvers' shortsightedness. Thank you, Lord, for the shy violet and bless all those who are blooming without recognition even though the world has given them the wrong name. Weed indeed!

A Breezy Blossom

Sometimes known as the wind flower, the anemone has several names and is associated with several legends. The botanical name of the anemone comes from Greek words that mean "wind" and "trembling." This name might have arisen because some anemones bloom very early in the spring and have no shelter so the slightest breeze makes their flowering heads seem to tremble. Possibly they were called wind flowers because anemones grew in windy places or because they were thought to only flower when the wind blew.

Another name for the anemone is the pasque flower because some anemones bloomed near Passion Week. And there was once a legend that anemones were the "lilies of the field" mentioned in the Bible. Another legend says that the petals of the wild anemones were red because the blood from Christ's cross dripped on them.

Whatever the legends or the names, the anemone is a sprightly flower that comes in several colors and different species. Some bloom in early spring, others in mid spring to summer, others from summer to mid fall. So you just might see an anemone any time!

The name anemone rolls off the tongue in a way that makes me laugh, Lord, but so do lots of other names like Lulubelle and falafel and paleontology and mellifluous. As you can see, Lord, it doesn't take much to make me giggle. Thank you for that. It makes some wonder why I'm so silly but it makes others giggle along with me.

With sprightly flowers and legends and a gentle breeze in the air, who wouldn't giggle. I think I'll meditate on this flower name today… anemone…anemone…anemone…. Are you giggling, Lord?

There's a Lion on My Lawn!

The fancy French name for a small yellow flower is *dent de lion* and some call it the Shepherd's Clock and we know it as the dandelion. But if you've ever tried to evict it from your lawn, you may wish you didn't know it at all.

The French name means "a lion's tooth" because of the dandelion's jagged, tooth-shaped leaf. It's called the shepherd's clock because in fields where shepherds keep watch, the dandelion flower opens when the sun rises and closes when the sun is ready to set. And people once believed that if you plucked a white feathery dandelion seed head and blew on it three times, the number of seeds left would tell you the hour of the day.

Well, if you don't want those dandelion seeds spread all over your lawn, do *not* blow. Forget the shepherd's clock and use your own clock to find out what time it is!

Actually, this plant/weed has its uses. Its leaves are often picked to use in salads or to brew a sparkling wine. The Romans made a medicine from its roots which they used to treat rheumatism. Birds feast on its seeds and carry off its soft silky fluff for a nest mattress.

And the dandelion has a hidden secret. It *looks* like one flower but if you examine it with a magnifying glass, you'll see as many as two hundred teeny-tiny flowers joined together to make this a dandy lion!

Lord, even though I don't like it in my lawn, I can't help but admire this little plant. No matter how you smash it, bash it, or insult it, it struggles to keep on growing and soon pops right back, showing you a cheery smile as bright as the morning sun. Lord, teach me to be like the dandelion. Even when I feel mistreated, I can sometimes rise above it—but not always with a smile. Help me to muster my teeny-tiny grit and gumption so I can trade in those victim pouts for dandelion smiles.

Mirror, Mirror on the Wall...

Beauty is in the eye of the beholder, and one large flowering bush must have really caught the eye of one beholder—because he named it beauty bush. In a cottage garden, this cold-hardy bush blooms in early spring with masses of misty pink flowers and then makes a nice background for later-blooming summer flowers. But the botanist who introduced the beauty bush to America was not a stay-in-the-background kind of guy.

Frank Meyer was a colorful, adventurous man who once walked from Holland to Italy just to see the orange groves (and nearly died in the Alps on the way). His expeditions were often sponsored by the U. S. Department of Agriculture and, in addition to flowers, he sent hundreds of food plants back to America, including eighteen varieties of soy beans! He was fascinated by plant diseases and economically useful plants but, unlike most botanists, did not have a great love of flowers. Maybe after he found the beauty bush, he lost interest in all other flowers. Who knows!

Mirror, mirror on the wall, is the beauty bush the fairest of them all? In the garden, there is no fairest. Each flower, each plant, has a special place, a special beauty—just like each person. Lord, help me to remember that and look for the beauty even in the not-so-obviously beautiful.

And always remind me that beauty is as beauty does....

Cardiac Arrest

The name of the pretty bleeding heart flower sounds like it needs to call 911 or to head for the hospital right away. But it doesn't. This is one of the best-loved old-fashioned perennial garden plants. Its strings of tiny red hearts and lush greenery make a striking display when planted with other spring-blooming plants.

This flower is one of many discovered by the British botanist, Robert Fortune, who encountered a few mis-fortunes to get it! When a treaty was signed in 1842 that allowed plant collectors to enter China for the first time, Fortune set out to explore that then-unknown world. With only a Chinese dictionary and some glass plant cases, he was able to collect some of our greatest garden treasures.

Then, to enter the still-forbidden *interior* of China, he disguised himself with Chinese clothing and a fake Chinese "pigtail" of braided hair. This led to many adventures and mis-fortunes. He fell into a wild boar trap, was chased by angry crowds, got robbed, and fought off a pirate attack. In spite of all this, Fortune smuggled out many plants to send to Europe, introduced the kumquat to England, and his experiments led to the growing of tea in India.

Well! Who knew it would take such heroics to get a tiny spring blossom into my garden. I'm glad I can just go down to the nearest garden store and bring home all the plants I can afford—although a trip to China does sound exciting.

Lazy, lazy have I become, Lord. I like to read about adventures but that's as far as I get. Oh well, maybe I'll read enough to find out how to smuggle some adventurous plants into that one little corner by the house where nothing seems to want to dig in and put its heart into growing there. Help me, Lord, to be a bit more adventurous and a lot more adaptable so I, too, can learn how to dig in and put my heart into growing wherever I am planted.

Livin' in Clover

Where on earth did someone get the idea that if you are rich and enjoying a cushy life, you are living in clover? Well, it came from the idea that cows and bumblebees are lucky indeed to live in a field of clover since the sweet clovers are the favorite food of both cows and bumblebees! But the cow is the luckiest of the two because when the bumblebee sips the clover nectar, he also picks up pollen on his feet and buzzes away to spread pollen from flower to flower, making sure that the clover will keep blooming so he and the cow can continue "living in clover."

Now you've probably heard the legend that Saint Patrick used the three-in-one clover leaf to explain the Trinity, saying that God, like the leaf, is one and yet three-in-one—Father, Son, and Holy Spirit. And, of course, you know that if you are lucky enough to find a four-leaf clover, you must pick it and keep it with you—to bring you more luck. So perhaps if you were lucky enough to find a four-leaf clover on Saint Patrick's Day and you were wearing a green shirt and carrying a shamrock plant with you at the time, you would surely be so lucky, you would soon be living in clover!

Whee, Lord, ain't legends grand! It's fun to think about cows and bumblebees and clover and shamrocks in the month of March when we take time out to celebrate Saint Patrick's Day. And we should always take time out to celebrate and have fun. If we gardeners spend too much time sowing and mowing, seeding and weeding, we'll just spade away! (Sorry, Lord. I must have caught March madness.)

I Can't Believe It's Not Butter!

When I was a little girl, my mother called daffodils butter-cups so I grew up thinking that was their proper name. And then I found out that the buttercup is an almost-wildflower with blossoms that are cup-shaped and have the same bright yellow color as butter! In fact, farmers once believed that if a cow pasture had lots of buttercups growing in it, the cows who grazed there would produce butter that had the best yellow color!

There are several varieties of buttercups and surprisingly, all are poison—to a greater or lesser extent. They can even be dangerous to cattle if the cows happen to eat some of the variety known as the "cursed buttercup." But the cattle are perhaps a bit wiser than their owners (who like to see the yellow flowers in the fields) because the cows usually avoid those "cursed" blossoms.

Well, Lord, those bright yellow blossoms along a roadside or in a field look very pretty at a distance—just like some people in the media or in the news look very pretty and charming from a distance. But when you hear about their poisonous habits and lifestyles, they don't seem so attractive anymore. Yet these are often the very ones who become role models for the young and even the not-so-young. Yes, I'm afraid I, too, have been gullible enough at times to admire the un-admirable. Help me, Lord—help us all—to be like the smart cows and avoid people and habits that look good but are dangerous. Lead us into safer pastures.

April

The best place to seek God is in a garden.

You can dig for him there.

GEORGE BERNARD SHAW

Myrtle and Murtle

When I lived in the South, there were so many crape myrtle bushes growing everywhere that I was not impressed. I thought the crapes were creepy. Even though this backyard beauty made a spectacular appearance in full bloom, its crinkled and ruffled, purplish pink blossoms looked "old" or sad or something to me. Now I wish I could have a myrtle in my backyard but it gets too cold here for them to thrive. (Maybe I like them now because I, too, have gotten a bit crinkled and ruffled—though not sad and definitely not old—oh no!)

When my son was a teenager, he drove an old beat-up Volkswagen with a license plate that read "MURTLE." I thought "BUG-GY" would be more appropriate but maybe he had Murtle the Turtle in mind; then again, maybe he didn't, since I'm never sure *what* a teenager has in mind.

Every time I looked at my son's MURTLE license, I thought of those lovely crape myrtle bushes of my own teenage years and how I had misjudged them—as perhaps I sometimes misjudged him.

Yes, Lord, I get the message. Too often I don't want something until I can't have it. When I was surrounded with crape myrtles, I didn't like them. Now that I'd like to grow one, I can't. And the other message is that I should be more careful about my misjudging. I should move as slow as a turtle before I make a judgment but be quicker to recognize beauty when I come across it. Murtle and Myrtle, I salute you!

Good Morning to You!

If the dawn comes up like thunder, so does the morning glory. It blooms in the early morning and goes to sleep in the afternoon. But what a lovely sight it makes when it's awake. A lady who loves blue once sat under an arbor covered with blooming blue morning glories and said she would never forget it because it looked as though someone had cut out a piece of the morning sky and put it in the garden.

These blue beauties with their heart-shaped leaves have a habit of winding their way into your heart—and over your fence and around a trellis and up your garden wall. But the morning glory winds in only one direction. Regardless of its location—in your backyard or a different city or a different country—each morning glory is "programmed" to never vary the direction it takes when it starts wending its way up a support.

No wonder the morning glory gets an early start—it already knows which way it's going to go so it doesn't need to waste time looking at a map and it doesn't have to ask a friend if it would be better to wind to the right or to the left. It doesn't even need one of those new gadgets that they put in cars to tell you where you are and which way to go from there. What a sense of direction!

Lord, I wish I was like the morning glory, knowing exactly which way to grow. I also wish I could afford a new gadget-filled car—but even if I could, I don't think it would help me find which way I should go from here or which corner I should turn next. Only you can do that, Lord, and sometimes you give confusing directions. Could you be a little more specific, Lord? You used to send burning bushes and instructions carved in stone. Have you considered e-mail?

The Dandelion Corsage

The lovely camellia is a relative of the tea plant and traveled from China to England to America in the late eighteenth century. Today it grows lushly here in warm-climate gardens, but I first encountered it in a downtown department store.

When I was a teenager, malls were not in style but going downtown to shop was. Sometimes my mother and I or my friends and I would spend half a day wandering down the aisles of department stores, looking for nothing but examining everything.

For some strange reason, one of the stores began "importing" California camellias each Saturday. They would be carefully arranged in long white boxes, swaddled in thin damp sheets of cotton. You would lift the cotton and feast on the colors and shadings. Some were pure pink or salmon or deep rose. Some were almost white with thin stripes of red or pink. All were exotically beautiful.

Since they were also very inexpensive, I would bring one home, tie a ribbon on it, and wear the "corsage" to church on Sunday, pretending that Prince Charming had presented it to me the night before. I may have looked silly but I felt fabulous.

Years later, I was in California for a special occasion that required a corsage and I asked if I might have a camellia corsage. They looked at me aghast and said, "That would be like wearing a dandelion corsage. Camellias grow everywhere here." I settled for pink carnations.

Lord, it's funny how silly memories linger. I remember the camellias but forgot where I parked the car. Jog my brain, Lord, and help me remember to say my prayers and do good deeds and floss my teeth and get milk at the Quick Shop since I forgot it at the grocery. And, Lord, I know it's silly since I never even see a camellia anymore and my garden is too cold-natured to welcome one—but some day, somehow, I want another camellia corsage.

Poached Eggs and Baby-Blues

What a combination! The only thing these two interesting flowers have in common is the fact that they were both discovered by the same botanist—a Scottish explorer who wandered around the world with his scraggly little dog seeking new flower specimens to introduce to Europe. He came across the two plants he called baby-blue-eyes and poached eggs when he was on a trip to the damp northwest coast of America—so these two delicate garden flowers are not sun lovers. They do well in misty English gardens today but, unlike the English gentlemen of song, they do not come out in the midday sun!

True to their name, the blue flowers are the clear bright blue of a baby's eyes. The yellow and white poached egg flowers also faintly resemble their namesake. This plant covers itself with lots of blossoms—and those blossoms are usually covered with lots of bees. (Who would guess that bees would like poached eggs!)

Lord, thank you for poached eggs and baby-blue eyes and bees and botanists who had the imagination and creativity to plant so many ear-catching names on plants. I smile every time I think about these two. And it's good to smile in the garden—or anywhere. I am reminded that plants are beautiful but they can't smile or laugh like I can. So thank you, Lord, for still another blessing—a sense of humor and the gift of laughter.

The Gold Rush

L ong before the gold rush—when everyone raced to California to search for golden treasure—Spanish explorers named California the "Golden West" because of its hills of wildly blooming yellow poppies!

The California poppy opens in the morning, closes at night, and spreads gold wherever it blooms. We usually hear about botanists bringing plants from other parts of the world to introduce them to America but this poppy was taken from America to Russia by a botanist named Chamisso when he joined an around-the-world expedition in 1815 after the end of the Napoleonic Wars. The sun-loving California poppy might not have appreciated being transplanted that way but, then again, this poppy might have welcomed the adventure because it looks fragile but blooms generously and actually prefers poor, sandy soil.

I've noticed that sometimes the most fragile looking people can bravely face the storms of suffering and sadness and quietly triumph. The same is true of gardeners. During World War II, people of all ages got out their shovels and planted "Victory Gardens" of vegetables to help the war effort and today again, people of all ages are pitching in to claim victory in troubled neighborhoods. They are "adopting" neglected lots and working together to clean them up and then plant vegetables and flowers. They turn empty spots into minigardens to bring pride and beauty to the streets where they live.

Lord, this again proves that you don't have to join an around-the-world expedition to find good hardworking folks and hometown heroes. They may be young or old or have fragile support systems but they withstand stormy seas and survive and thrive as an example to others. Bless them all.

Herb Who?

What would a garden be without a few herbs? And there are plenty of interesting ones. There are hundreds of varieties of thyme with scents and flavors ranging from lemon to caraway and, in the age of chivalry, thyme was an emblem of courage. That's why ladies embroidered thyme sprigs on scarves for their knights to wear into battle. The leaves of the herb borage have a cool cucumber flavor, and its seeds contain a type of acid that is used to treat those with circulatory disorders. The herb tarragon lends flavor to stews, butter, and vinegar, but it was once used to cure the bites of mad dogs!

Today sage is best known as an ingredient for turkey stuffing, but in ancient times it was thought to confer long life! It was also one of the aromatic "strewing" herbs that were strewn on the floor so that a pleasant scent would arise when you walked on them. King James II even had a "royal strewer!"

And herbs were once used to pay taxes! Yep! They were once as good as money because of their healing and aromatic uses. Four "tithing herbs" are mentioned in the Bible—dill, cumin, mint, and rue.

Lord, today if you tried to pay your tax bill with a bunch of herbs, you would be told to "Go directly to jail and do not collect two hundred dollars!" Of course, herbs are still valuable—to add beauty to your garden and flavor to your cooking. And there's one that I grew up with and must have in my garden—the memorable mint. There are over six hundred varieties of mint, and I do love it—in iced tea and green peas and even in a bouquet. But, Lord, if you give it an inch, it will take over your whole garden. I wish I was as indestructible as that pretty, flavory mint. But since I'm not, give me courage, protect my circulatory system, save me from mad dogs, remind me to pick up that stuff strewn on my floor, and please help me pay my taxes. Thanks. Amen.

Hello, Funny Face

Smiling through spring is a sure thing if you have a pot of pansies on the patio. Every time you pass them, those funny little faces are smiling up at you—and each one is different. There's the shy purple, the deep purple, the white with a purple smile, the sunshine yellow, the yellow with a purple scowl—every time you look, you see a different face. It's just like you're sitting at the mall waiting to meet someone and you start to people-watch. Each face is so different from the one that just passed by.

Pansies always remind me of the endless mystery of God's creation. Making so many flowers and plants and animals and insects is a mind-boggling accomplishment—but faces! What a challenge. Think about it. The "canvas" is so small. A face is only a few inches across and a few inches high. And there are only two eyes, two ears, one nose, one mouth, a couple of eyebrows, some eyelashes, and some skin to work with. Yet each one has been a bit different since the dawn of peoplekind!

I even run out of ideas about what to fix for dinner. There are only so many combinations of meat, pasta, and vegetables; and after three hundred sixty-five days, I have to start over. But those faces! Every time a new baby arrives, there's a new combination of eyes, ears, and noses! It's divine!

Lord, Lord, they say pansies are for thoughts and these are my thoughts of today. I've been wanting to ask you about your face factory for a long time, but I knew you wouldn't tell me the secret. Making dinner should be easier than making faces but evidently it isn't. You never run out of ideas! I am very impressed and I continue to be amazed by the endless variety of your creations every day. But I really must stop chatting now. I have to figure out what to fix for dinner.

Wistfully Misspelled

The lovely climbing plant known as wisteria is wistfully flaunting a misspelled name! It was originally named after Caspar Wistar, a professor, distinguished botanist, president of the Philosophical Society, and friend of Thomas Jefferson!

Obviously, Dr. Wistar traveled in important circles and was known in "high places" and his namesake follows his example by climbing to high places atop a patio, porch, or arbor. Although the professor might be academically shocked that the "a" in his name somehow got changed to an "e," he would surely be proud of this beautiful vine.

Looking romantically picturesque and filling the air with a gentle fragrance, lavender or white wisteria blossoms bend gracefully down in long swags and soften the view wherever they grow. And after the blooms fade the bright greenery provides dense summertime shade.

I know just how it feels to be misspelled, Lord. My maiden name of McCarver was always being misspelled as McCraver. I do crave chocolate but I didn't like being labeled as a chronic craver. Then I married and changed my name to one I thought would have no problem with spelling. Wrong! All too often I get envelopes addressed to Mrs. Synder—which sounds an awful lot like sinner. It seems I have a knack of going from bad to worse. But what's in a name, Lord? What's in a name? The wisteria has "risen above" its missplaced letter. Help me, too, to rise above my craving and synning so there'll be no room for wistfulness in my garden.

Barbara's Buttons, Queen Anne's Lace, and Black-Eyed Susan

Who *are* all those flowery ladies? Well, if you'll pardon the expression, they're wildflowers—but very nice ones. And their names are welcome on the invitation list to any garden party.

Barbara's buttons are ball-shaped clusters of dainty, fragrant white flowers. And surely you've met those golden daisy-like flowers with the black-eyed centers. Susan is a regular in lots of gardens. But Queen Anne's lace is an "it depends" plant. To the unimaginative, it is a weed to be avoided. Others think its lovely lacy flowers and ferny foliage make a graceful addition to the garden and also to bouquets— even bridal bouquets. Sometimes—whether it's a plant or a person—the beauty of a friend is all in the eye of the beholder.

Some day, Lord, I'm going to have a real garden party and wear a big hat and serve lemon cake and tall icy drinks and make a big bouquet of Barbara's buttons, Queen Anne's lace, and black-eyed Susans as the centerpiece for the cake table. Actually, through the years, I've had some really good friends named Barbara, Anne, and Susan and when we got together, we were sometimes a little bit wild—but only with laughter. It's great to have friends who will laugh with you and cry with you—and know how to turn some of your cries into laughs, your sads into glads. Thanks, Lord, for all the wildflowers and the little-bit-wild friends—in years past, days present, and on-the-way future.

Parslied Petunias?

Sure, you've heard of parslied potatoes but parslied petunias? In early America, gardeners usually grew rows of vegetables alongside rows of flowers and today the trend is returning. Gardeners are planting frilly parsley with the petunias, beets by the begonias and feathery asparagus with asters. Early "red sails" lettuce and spring green onions can fill a spot and be harvested for your salad bowl in time to make way for some colorful summer annuals.

Scarlet runner beans are often grown today as ornamental plants instead of vegetables because they make such a pretty picture with their red flowers, long green-bean pods, and fluttering leaves. And many gardening books now show designs for planting herbs, vegetables, and flowers all together to make a multi-patterned, multi-colored design as variegated as an early American quilt.

That early American, Thomas Jefferson, was famous for his gardens of flowers and vegetables. One of his favorites was the curly purple and yellow snail-flower bean, which Jefferson described as "the most beautiful bean in the world." Today's Center for Historical Plants at Thomas Jefferson's Monticello issues a catalog that includes a combination of such items as the Blackberry-lily and McMahon's Texas Bird pepper, English lavender and Brandywine tomato, Sensitive plant (whose leaves curl up to the touch), Moon and Stars watermelon, and "Tennis Ball" lettuce.

Well, Lord, I have grown parsley and petunias, but I haven't had luck with many vegetables. When we moved to our current house, the former owners had a small garden full of tomatoes, peppers, and onions. We feasted that summer but when I tried to duplicate it the next year, my green thumb went thumbs down. The only thing I managed to combine was a hugely successful sweet potato plant that wandered all around some geraniums and was very pretty. But I do think combination is a great idea, Lord, just like a combination of people—with different ideas, insights, and talents—all contributing at work, at church, in the neighborhood. Thanks, Lord, for variety, for the differences that, if mixed right, can be as interesting as parslied petunias.

A Grass Bouquet

What? You say grass is not a flower? Maybe yes, maybe no. Did you know that of all the plants that grow on earth, grasses are the most important! And grass has seeds—so it "flowers"!

Why is grass so important? Grasses feed people and animals who live on the earth, so without grass, we'd be much hungrier. When you eat a slice of bread, it was made from flour that came from the seeds of wheat or rye—which are grasses. Rice is a grass—and so are corn, barley, oats. Sugar comes from sugarcane which is a grass. Pastures of grass feed sheep and cattle. And hay is dried grass that provides winter food for cows and horses. And birds feast on seeds from the grass family just like people do.

Grass feeds our bodies—and also our spirits. Aren't your spirits lifted when you view a green scene of grass that brightens parks, valleys, mountains, pastures, and prairies? Just think how ugly the earth would be if there was only brown, crusted dirt instead of that cheery green grass. And besides, it makes such a nice "frame" for your garden! So no matter how much trouble it may be to mow that lawn, give thanks for grass.

Lord, it is so easy to overlook the "expected" things we see every day and take them for granted. Who could imagine what life would be like without all those good things grasses give us? Of course, You could imagine and that's why you gave us grasses. Forgive us, Lord, when we stupidly complain about how much trouble it is to care for the gifts you give us—whether it's a crying baby, a troublesome teen, or a lawn that needs mowing.

May

*Floriculture…while being health giving is also
a pure and harmless recreation, which may be engaged
in by individuals of either sex and of all stations of life,
the peasant as well as the peer, the overtoiled man
of business and the industrious artisan,
on every imaginable scale from a
single flower pot to the princely conservatory.*

BANBURY GUARDIAN (1866)

A Rose Is a Rose Is a Strawberry?

The rose family is a wild and crazy one—maybe even more confusing than mine or yours! Since the name *rose* comes from the Latin word for "red," you might first think of those lush red long-stemmed beauties or the bright red summer bloomers that climb over a backyard fence—but that's just the beginning. Roses are like our own "extended" families. They come in many colors, sizes, and shapes. Some grow in hothouses; others wander wildly across fields, scramble through hedges, or make themselves at home in your own backyard. And some have only a slight family resemblance—like the flower of the strawberry plant. Yes, believe it or not, the strawberry also belongs to the rose family.

Roses even wander beyond the garden! You can find them in art museum paintings, on wall paper, wrapping paper, summer skirts and winter house shoes. And many have been given fanciful names like All That Jazz, Chrysler Imperial, Popcorn, and Empress Josephine.

Napoleon's Empress Josephine was famous for her rose gardens and *always* carried a fresh rose with her. Can you guess why? She held the rose over her mouth when she smiled—to hide her bad teeth! (Guess they didn't have a friendly family dentist in her day.)

Thank you, Lord, for all the wild and crazy families—of roses and of people. Thank you, too, for dentists and the wonderful person who invented the dentists' painkilling novocaine. You know, Lord, that I'm afraid of painful surprises, from the dentist or from a rose thorn in my bouquet of days. Yet I know others have much worse pains to face. Help them, Lord. And help me to be braver on those days when a rose is a rose is a thorn.

The King's Flower

When I was growing up in Tennessee, irises grew in everybody's backyard and we called them flags. Kids brought bouquets of them to teachers, and irises were used to decorate the church altars. Walking to school, I passed an empty lot that was just full of all kinds of irises so this flower was too everyday for me to appreciate it.

Now I know that the iris was the symbol of the kings of France and this "flag" flew on their flags! Irises were on King Louis VII's banner during the Second French Crusade and were called fleur de Louis—which became the fleur-de-lis, which is sometimes used as a symbol for the city of St. Louis, which is where I live now! How about that!

The iris plant has been popular in many countries for many years. It was grown in early European gardens and was carved as a symbol on Egypt's famous Temple of Karnak near the Nile. And, back in the days when they wore powdered wigs (you may have seen someone wearing one in a movie), dried ground iris roots were used to produce violet-scented orris root which was used to powder those wigs! So—my "everyday" flower turns out not to be so "everyday" after all.

Here I am, found stupid again, Lord! Maybe it wasn't too bad for a kid to not get excited about an everyday flower called a flag even if it was as beautiful as the exotic orchid—but by now I should have wised up. Sorry to say, Lord, that I still sometimes take everyday miracles for granted—neglecting to get excited about a cool glass of water, fresh lettuce for my salad, sunshine for my morning, rain for my garden, and everyday friends that are beautiful though not always exotic. Send up the flag, Lord, and this time, I'll salute.

You Are My Sunshine

Mary, Mary, never contrary, how does your garden grow? A pretty little yellow flower that is a regular in many gardens got its name from "Mary's gold" because it has long been associated with Mary, the mother of Jesus—possibly because the marigold loves the sun as Mary loved the Son. A gardener's delight, the humble little marigold is easy to grow—and never contrary. It holds its head up and smiles at the noonday sun while other plants are wilting away, begging for some shade and a drink of water.

Did you know the original European marigold was once called "calendula" from a Latin word that meant "the first day of the month"? That's because it bloomed *every* month of the year in some monastery gardens and constantly supplied flowers to decorate the church altars.

Lord, I'm sorry to say that, unlike the marigold, I am one of the wilters. Sometimes I will boldly make a statement, full of vim and vigor—but the moment someone challenges me about my "facts," I begin to falter and question. Did I really remember the right quote or the proper date or who said what when? Even when I'm sure I know what I'm talking about, I sometimes have to take a step back before I take a step forward. Oh, I know you know I'm not always right and I should be willing to admit that but when I am right, I should be willing to admit that too! So help me, Lord, to get my head better organized so I can be sure of what I'm going to say before I've said it. Then, instead of wilting, I can be a marigold and hold my head up to the sun—and the Son—and smile.

The Teary-Eyed Fritillary

The frilly fritillary produces nodding flower bells in an unusual variety of patterns, sizes, and shapes. Unlike most flowers, these blossoms are often striped, speckled, or checkered in a range of watercolor hues. And if you touch a petal, it will sometimes weep a small "tear" from the reservoir of nectar that is at the base of each petal.

The plants range from the bold, imposing crown imperial which produces a garland of bright blossoms on tall, strong stalks to a small, dainty woodland species that has single modest flowers on slim stems. But the one that interests me most is the guinea-hen fritillary which has a speckled pattern similar to the speckles of a guinea hen's feathers. Now you might wonder how I know about a guinea hen's feathers—so I'll tell you.

When I was a kid, we often visited an aunt and uncle who lived on a farm. I remember the pies made from the cherries on their trees. And I remember the guineas. They seemed very exotic to me. And of course, we sometimes had roast guinea for dinner. I never forgot that because we *never* had roast guinea at home. Now I know the farm guinea is related to the fancy pheasant just like the guinea-hen fritillary is related to the imposing crown imperial fritillary. Whether fowls, flowers, or folks, family trees are amazing!

There are so many amazing family trees mentioned in the Bible, Lord—and my own tree has broad branches with distant cousins occasionally showing up to happily surprise me. If it hadn't been for that one and only family farm connection, I never would have known about guineas and I wouldn't have been so delighted to discover the guinea-hen fritillary. Thanks, Lord, for so many frilling surprises!

The Old Man's Beard

Now who would call a show-stopping fragrant flower an "old man's beard?" This flower's nickname must have come from the fact that the beautiful clematis flower has masses of feathery seed heads that evidently reminded some botanist of a beard!

Through the years, other botanists have had some other strange ideas about how to grow this spectacularly flowered plant. The clematis is a vine, but one botanist suggested that you "peg down" the vines so they would grow across the ground and fill flower beds. Another suggested you should let the clematis grow through and around a bush so it would look like you had thrown a "veil" over the bush.

The clematis survived the name and the suggestions and now vines happily on light posts, trellises, and mail boxes—and looks breathtakingly beautiful.

Lord, it seems lots of people always have "good" suggestions about how something or someone else should "grow"! They know just how you should decorate your house, raise your children, and grow your garden. Where do they get such a strange idea? What's that you say, Lord? Well, okay, maybe I'm one of the ones who can sometimes be a little too generous with my advice. So help me, Lord, to stop throwing out veiled remarks—and some that are not so veiled—and then all my friends can be breathtakingly surprised.

How Could You Forget?

As Shakespeare said, "...rosemary—that's for remembrance." This flowering herb has many uses and is the subject of many legends. Because it is known as the herb of fidelity and remembrance, it has often been included in bridal bouquets *and* in funeral sprays. It has been used as a hair rinse and an air freshener and bunches of it were once burned to try to drive away the plague!

One of the most popular legends tells that when the Holy Family was fleeing into Egypt, Mary draped her blue cloak over a white flowering rosemary bush one night—and the next morning, the flowers had turned blue. There is still one type of rosemary with white flowers but most of them flower in shades of blue. That's the reason that this herb is also known as the pilgrim's plant.

Another legend says that the rosemary will never grow taller than a man and will never live longer than thirty-three years, the number of years Christ lived on earth.

But the idea that caught my attention was that you could weave a garland of rosemary and wear it in your hair to improve your memory. If I did that, maybe I could better remember names, dates, appointments, and the need to pick up milk and bread at the grocery before I casually head home to read a book.

Yes, Lord, I am easily distracted so I often say to myself, "How could you forget that?" I guess you say that a lot too, Lord, when I forget to say a single prayer on a busy day or neglect to send a get-well or sympathy card to one of your suffering children. Sorry, Lord, I'll try to do better. In fact, I'll start today. I'll go out and buy a rosemary plant so I'll have it ready ahead of time to give as a gift to someone who needs one—if I remember.

Sweet Surprise

The plant in my patio garden that is the prettiest, showiest, most healthy—and most aggravating—is one I did *not* plant. Some visiting bird must have dropped some seeds a few years ago and, to my surprise, I suddenly had some lovely colorful wild sweet peas growing where they had not been expected.

I was so pleased when they started blooming and spreading all over the place. Everyone oohed and aahed at their beauty. And the next year, without me doing a thing, they reappeared and were beautiful again but this time they had reseeded themselves so efficiently that they took over, crowding out all the other plants. I tried to train them up a trellis and they cooperated but that didn't stop them from continuing to grow under the trellis, under the fence, and over the sidewalk. Finally I had to start pulling up the vines and discarding them by the bagful.

Ever since, this wild sweet pea and I have had a love-hate relationship. I love the flowers and there are always plenty to bring in the house for bouquets when nothing else is blooming, but I have to protect my other plants from getting smothered. So what's a gardener to do!

Actually, Lord, I think I feel closer to this plant than any other because I also have been known to go for too much of a good thing. My hall is filled with framed pictures of so many relatives, I'm afraid the plaster may give up and cave in some day. When company comes, I might fix two desserts instead of one and I sometimes wear three kinds of beads when one would do just fine. Like the sweet pea, I start out okay but then go wild and get carried away—so help me to learn, Lord, that sometimes less is best.

Granny's Bonnet

The pretty little columbine is sometimes called granny's bonnet because it's shaped a bit like an old-fashioned bonnet that grandmas once wore. And a bunch of columbines all in bloom, nodding together in the wind, might remind you of a group of bonnetted ladies nodding and gossiping over the back fence.

The wild columbine has graceful two-foot stems with dainty, nodding crimson and yellow bonnet blossoms from spring to midsummer. But there are several species of columbines, and they don't all wear the same bonnets. In old paintings and tapestries (I know not why!) the columbine was seen as something much more serious than a bonnet. It was used to represent the dove of peace, the symbol of the Holy Spirit.

Well, Lord, you may remember that my grandma really did wear a bonnet when she went "out back" to tend her garden or feed her chickens. She was some kind of lady! As a girl she had "poor health" and the doctor urged my grandpa to move the family from Indiana to warmer Tennessee. This fragile flower had seven children, grew all her own vegetables, and "put them up" for the winter, raised chickens and a cow, milked the cow, churned butter, and made the best homemade biscuits in town.

Since her time, I have known lots of modern grandmas who never did any of those things and never wore a bonnet—but are just as wonderful. In fact, they aren't even called "granny" or "grandma." They have names like Gemma, Gigi, Mondee, and Nana. So grandmas by any other name can be just as sweet. (It was suggested to my grandson that he call me Nana but he pronounced it Bana—which was the same name he used for bananas and that seemed appropriate!—so I've been Bana ever since.) Thank you, Lord, for grandmas and columbines and all such blessings that brighten our lives, no matter how we name them!

Lend an Ear

D ramatic as a cyclone but not as noisy, the cyclamen quietly blooms with dainty, distinctive flowers that rise on slender stems from a clump of marbled gray and green leaves. The petals of the cyclamen are sometimes double, ruffled, shredded, or ridged so they look like exotic butterflies. But during the Renaissance, it was the plant's leaves that got attention.

At that time, there was much philosophical discussion among scholars about everything—including plants and medicine. One distinguished doctor decreed that you could judge by the appearance of a plant why it had been created. He thought the cyclamen leaf looked like an ear so it should be used to treat earache!

Whenever anything ear-shaped is mentioned, I become self-conscious because I inherited what is known as the McCarver ear. I have an old photograph of my father with his father and the two of them have ears that look like they could surely take flight in a strong wind. Some families pass down art treasures and valuable antiques. Mine passed on ears—to me and several other lucky heirs. Every time I get a haircut, I caution the cutter to be sure to leave enough hair to cover the ears and no one ever suggests that's not necessary.

It's fascinating and still a mystery, Lord, as to why you made things the way you did—and why you made me an ear heir! But at least I'm glad I didn't live in the Renaissance because it would have taken a lot of cyclamen leaves to cure one of my ears. Maybe my family trait should remind me to listen carefully, to lend an ear to those who have troubles to share, to be all ears when Scripture is being discussed, to keep it to myself when I get an earful of gossip, and keep my ear to the ground for signs of trouble so I can stop family rumbles before they start. Hmmm….that sounds like a pretty big order—so don't be surprised, Lord, when I bend your ear in prayer, asking for help.

At Your Service...

D o you sometimes feel that you're always busy "doing" or "serving" here or there—entertaining, volunteering, helping out, or welcoming in? Do you wish sometimes *you* could get some service? Well, how about planting a serviceberry in your backyard? Then you could look out your kitchen window and delight in knowing you have a beautiful friend who is also labeled "at your service!"

This small tree or shrub has lovely clusters of dangling white or pinkish flowers in early spring—and makes a wonderful rest stop for the birds. Maybe that's why it's called a "service" berry. It's a service station/motel that also provides food. It has tiny berries in the summer that have a nutty blueberry flavor that birds—and people— love. The berries are delicious in pies, muffins, or jelly—if you ever get to pick them before the birds do!

Strangely, the serviceberry is known by different names in different parts of the country. It is also known as shadblow, shadbush, Juneberry, and Saskatoon! But doesn't that seem appropriate for one in "service"? I, too, am known by many names—and I bet you are too. I'm a wife, mom, aunt, friend, cook, dustball collector, grocery shopper, news reporter, and, of course, gardener.

Lord, some days I want to go AWOL *and leave the service for a few days. I want to complain about "other people" taking up all my time and energy. I want to whine and resign and recline. But then I think about how lucky I am that I can be of service to others—and to you. I realize service must be tempered with prudence and there are times I should say, "Sorry but no"—and times when I should offer "service with a smile." Lord, help me to know when to say no and when to say yes. Teach me to keep my whines to myself and blossom like the serviceberry.*

June

This very act of planting a seed in the earth

has in it to me something beautiful.

I always do it with a joy

that is largely mixed with awe.

CELIA THAXTER

Love Me, Love Me Not

Generations of children have loved the bright white-petaled, yellow-centered flower sometimes called the day's-eye. And when I was a little girl, there was a game we played that I think maybe little girls still play. If you liked a boy in your class and you wondered if he liked you too, you would pick a daisy, pluck off one white petal and say, "He loves me." Then you would pluck off another petal and say, "He loves me not," and you would continue plucking until you came to the last petal. If that was a "He loves me" petal, you smiled a secret smile. If it was "He loves me not," you found another daisy and tried again!

The daisy is sometimes even called the "love me-love me not" flower and is popular all over the world. The daisy probably originated in China and traveled in the holds of ships to Europe and then to America. Maybe the Pilgrims accidentally brought the seeds over in packing cases filled with hay. However they first came, the daisy seeds continued to travel—on horse's hooves, in covered wagons, or railroad cars—all across the country. Today daisies are one of the most popular American garden flowers and make happy bouquets.

Everyone wants to be loved, Lord. And when you find out, "He loves me not" or "She loves me not" or "They love me not," it seems like the end of the world. But, thank goodness, daisies don't tell the truth. There's always another chance, another corner to turn, another daisy to pluck. Help me, Lord, on days when I feel unloved and unlovable. And help me even more, Lord, on days when I make someone else feel that way. Teach me to never do that again.

Dahling, It's a Dahlia!

Identifying a dahlia could be confusing since a dahlia can be as large as a dinner plate or as small as an appetizer! They come in quite a variety of shapes, sizes, and colors. The bambino white dahlia has one-inch flowers. The collarette has a central disk with a ruffled collar. The jack-o-lantern has an inner collar streaked yellow and orange. The pompoms produce small round balls of tightly curled petals. But whatever shape or size, this is a long-lasting cut flower that makes dahling dahlia bouquets!

There's also a dahling dahlia story. It seems that many years ago, a Frenchman was sent to Mexico to smuggle out some special insects that were carefully guarded by the Mexican government because they were a precious source of red dye. The Frenchman managed to get a good supply of the insects, put them in a box of dahlias so they would have food for the journey, and shipped them off to France. When the box arrived, the insects were dead because a dahlia diet did not suit them but the long-lasting dahlias were just fine.

That's the way it goes, Lord. I buy a bunch of exotic food that looks great and smuggle it onto the dinner table and nobody wants to touch the stuff because it isn't part of their "usual" diet. It doesn't look like pizza or any other staff of life and they'd rather die than try it. Well, I'm just as guilty. I see those great TV exercise shows but those movements don't look like my usual way of slouching along so I don't want to try it. Forgive us all, Lord, for loving the ruts we've gotten stuck in. Help us to try variety the way the dahlia does. Remind us that "the usual" might not be the spice of life.

Don't Needle the Pincushion

If you've ever been on pins and needles looking for an easy-to-grow workhorse for the garden, look no further. It's the pincushion flower! There's no long story or secret about how this plant got its name. When you meet it in a garden, you'll know. It has fluffy petals and in their center, there's a bunch of stamens that stick up and look just like straight pins stuck in a pincushion!

Now a pincushion can be very beautiful but it's also sort of a quiet workaday household item—and so is this flower. It blooms in several colors, requires little care, has long-lasting flowers from spring to fall, grows happily in a "cutting" garden, and makes a lovely addition to a fresh arrangement. It may not be as famous as some of the showier flowers but it sure has a great work record.

Lord, I have a friend who is attractive, has a nice family, a pretty home, a good job, and is always available when someone needs a helping hand. Yet she is not satisfied with herself. She keeps saying she has not done anything "important," and no matter how much her friends try to reassure her, she still sees herself as a failure. I guess a lot of people have that feeling. In spite of their great "work record," they feel "less" than their showier friends or relatives. Help them, Lord, to see themselves the way their friends do and the way you do—as a beautiful and important part of your garden. Ease their worry so they can realize how valuable they are and stop always being on pins and needles.

Up, Up, and Away...

Have you ever had a wild desire to fly up, up, and away in a hot-air balloon but didn't have the nerve—or the money? Well, here's a plan: plant some balloon flowers and when they're in bud, you can tell yourself that even though you haven't left on your flight yet, you might fly away at any moment—because your balloon is parked just outside in the garden.

This plant got its happy name because its bud is bulbous like a blown-up balloon ready to celebrate a birthday or decorate a party! And when this balloon pops into bloom, the flower is a lovely blue— a treasure for gardeners since there are so few blue flowers. (The flower also comes in pink or white and they're nice too—but not as rare as blue!)

Lord, I do love balloons—both the flower ones and the big hot-air ones and the little blowup ones that you tie on a mailbox to let people know this is where to stop for the get-together!

In the town where I live they have a hot-air balloon race every year and the night before the race, people bring picnic lunches and sit in a field to watch workers firing up the balloons, preparing for the race. The huge colored balloons fill with light from the fire so they call it a "balloon glow"—and it is a lovely sight to see in the dark night.

That's the way I feel sometimes, Lord, when you speak to me through the sight of a beautiful flower or the company of a beautiful person. I feel the glow all inside. Thank you for those special moments and help me, Lord, to savor every moment you give me—the times when I feel as blue as the balloons that grow in the garden as well as the times when I feel as warm and joyful as the balloons that glow in the dark.

Into the Valley Again

I didn't mean to do it. I should have known better. I should have asked for help but I didn't. I'm so sorry but I think I mistreated my lily of the valley.

This is a plant that quietly sends up bright broad green leaves in the spring and then tiny white bell-shaped blossoms that have a heady aroma that I love. They were always blooming in my mother's yard so I brought some from Tennessee to Missouri and waited for them to take over. They flowered but did not flourish. When I moved to a new house, I dug them up and took them along but the lily of the valley did not like its new valley and died. I mourned its passing.

A few years later, a friend was thinning out her lily of the valley beds and offered me some. I was delighted and carefully planted them in a sunny spot. They struggled through the year but did not return in the spring. Again, another friend dug up some for me and I planted them in three different spots, hoping they would like one at least. They didn't. Finally, I got out the garden book and read that they needed shade, not sunshine! I don't remember my mother's plants being in the shade but I guess they liked her better than they did me!

In thinking of this plant, Lord, I realize that I may have also mistreated some people when I didn't mean to, didn't want to, and should have known better. Maybe they just wanted a little shade and I kept handing out sunshiny smiley faces. Maybe they just wanted peace and quiet and I kept offering conversation. No wonder they retreated. Help me, Lord, to pay attention and know when to step forward and when to step back, when to keep offering help or advice and when to just keep out of the way. But, Lord, I still want some lily of the valley blossoms in my garden so I planted a new batch—in a shady spot. Would you please tell them that if I make a mistake, I mean well. I just wanta be friends.

Busy Lizzie

There's a pot on my patio that overflows every summer with little pink, white, and red blossoms. The name of this plant, impatiens, seems appropriate because it looks like it just *can't wait* to bloom more and more. Every summer I've planted it and been rewarded by its profusion of color but it was just this year when I learned that in England, this plant is known as Busy Lizzie! What a friendly, fun name—and also appropriate since it keeps so busy spreading and blooming.

I've also learned that this plant literally shoots seeds from the pods to be sure they spread about and grow. There's even a little poem by Erasmus Darwin that says Busy Lizzie astonishes and alarms—when she "hurls her infants from her frantic arms."

This summer, Lord, I'm going to be having even more conversations than usual with this patio plant. I've always identified with one of her names since I am all too often impatient—just can't wait for the light to change, the job to get finished, the pot to boil. And now I have to admit that I'm also a Busy Lizzie, running around, trying to do too many things at once, hurling ideas and projects from my frantic arms. So, Lord, help me to curb my impatience and learn how to start only what my arms can finish—so my family and friends will be astonished instead of alarmed!

Make a Wish

O ne night when I was a little girl, my mother and I were sitting on the front steps on a warm Southern summer night, just doing nothing, just sitting in the secret dark night, smelling the honeysuckle in bloom. Suddenly, we saw a fiery streak across the sky. My mother jumped up and got all excited and said, "Make a wish." She said it was a magical thing when you saw a shooting star.

I don't remember my wish so I don't know if it came true, but I never forgot the magic feeling of that moment and I often remember it on a warm summer night when I'm just sitting, doing nothing, looking at the stars. And now I can remember it in the garden too, because there's a lovely wildflower named Southern shooting star.

It's a member of the primrose family but its blossom is quite distinctive. From a rosette of green leaves, a slim leafless stalk stands tall, topped with a tiny elegant bouquet of flowers with "upswept" petals. The bottom part of each flower looks almost like the pen point of an old fountain pen, pointing down, and from that, the petals grow straight up. You can either think the petals are shooting upward, reaching for the sky—or the penpoint is shooting down, with the petals streaking after it. Either way, I'm glad someone named it after "my" secret shooting star!

Lord, thanks for the memories. Thanks for all the gifts you've given us—the stars, the sky, the flowers, the mothers. They are all magical parts of life on this wonderful planet Earth.

All That Jazz

Jasmine has pretty yellow trumpet-like flowers and lush green-ery but its jazzy-est feature is its fragrance. The aroma is delicious but when in full bloom, the jasmine scent is so sweet, it can almost be overwhelming—like too many splashes of a jazzy perfume!

There are several varieties of this flower and they have been around a long time in a lot of places. The Chinese once combined dried jasmine blossoms with green tea to make an aromatic mixture called "Fragrant Leaves." Persians learned how to extract the jasmine scent by steeping the blossoms in sesame oil. And the English planted the jasmine on their arbors.

Jasmine grows beautifully on an arbor or trellis—with a little help. This plant has a "floppy" way of leaning on things because it needs to be supported or propped up *but* it politely does *not* twine itself around anything like a clinging vine. It needs you to guide it and waits for you to train it in the way you wish it to grow.

Oh, Lord, I need support, too, and some days I wish someone would prop me up in a corner before I collapse. But, unlike the lovely jasmine, I have also been guilty of clinging—hanging on to someone or something that I should set free, refusing to let go of an idea that needs to be replaced with a newer one. Lord, teach me to learn how to hold tight with open hands. Train me in the way you wish me to grow.

The "Mission" of Botanists

The name astilbe (as-TILL-bee) comes from the Greek words which mean "without brilliance" or "not shining," probably because an early type of this plant was pale and not very showy. Today's astilbes come in brilliant pink, red, white, or lilac and look like the feathery plumes that ladies once used to decorate those big "picture hats." The stalks vary from eight inches to four feet tall and when massed together in a garden can fill a shady spot with a shining bright cloud of color.

Today's astilbe is not a "without" flower and neither was the Jesuit missionary who found the astilbe in the Orient. Pere Armand David was sent to China to set up a school for boys, but he was such a dedicated botanist that he was allowed to take time away to collect plants—and he sent thousands of them back to Paris. Some of those plants are still known today by the botanical names that were given to them in his honor—like the beautiful davidia tree. He and other missionaries found many botanical treasures that were introduced into European gardens and later traveled around the world. The missionaries brought new faith to flower in a distant land and found new flowers to bring back to their homeland.

Well, Lord, we can't all be missionaries, but we can all teach and explore and find beauty in your flowers and all your creations. Help me to recognize and appreciate the wonder of both your plants and your people. And, Lord, remind me to be more careful about how I teach by example. Some of my bad habits do not teach a very good lesson to others. I may always be called "without brilliance" or "not shining," but I could at least try to achieve the title of "improved."

Sweet William Who?

No one seems to know why a pretty little pink flower is known as a pink but also as sweet William. It can't be named pink because of its color since this flower grew in Britain in the sixteenth century and it was not until the eighteenth century when there was a specific color named pink—so maybe the color got its name from the flower! Someone suggested it might be named after Saint William whose feast day is in June when this flower is blooming, but there are about a dozen Saint Williams, with feast days in almost every month of the year!

However it got its name, I like this flower because my husband, my nephew, and my grandson are all sweet Williams, and I had a wild and crazy relative named Uncle Pink (whose real name was Pinckney). Of course, the carnation is also part of this flower family, and I don't have any relatives named carnation. But the proper botanical family name for all three is dianthus, which comes from the Greek words meaning "divine flower." And that sounds like a blooming good family name to me!

Lord, my mother was a great seamstress, and she cut fabrics with a saw-toothed pair of pinking shears which made kind of a fancy pointed scallop or zigzag cut instead of a straight one. I was not allowed to touch those scissors for fear I would ruin them by cutting paper, which I wanted to do because I liked those jaggedy edges. And dianthus flowers have those same scallopy, jagged edges so maybe they were named after the pinking shears! But wait, no…probably the scissors were named after the flower. And now I'm wondering why "in the pink" means "in good health." Oh, well, wondering is good for the soul I guess and maybe it's good exercise for the brain—but right now, Lord, I've gotta quit exercising wonder and get out there and weed that garden so it too can stay "in the pink!"

July

*Arranging a bowl of flowers in the morning
can give a sense of quiet in a crowded day—
like writing a poem or saying a prayer.*

ANNE MORROW LINDBERGH

Moonstones and Blue Diamonds

One sunny afternoon my grown-up son took me for a ride near the ocean to show me a special place a friend had shown him—a meditation garden. We walked along shaded paths where the sun dappled lushly blooming azaleas and rhododendrons and plants that blossomed in a rainbow of gold, rose, crimson, and pure white. We went over small bridges and strolled past rippling waters where brilliantly colored fish swam and darted like watery jewels. The noise of the nearby highway was replaced by peace and tranquillity.

Water-worn rocks and gnarled trees spoke of timelessness. Waterfalls suggested continuity. Honeyed flower fragrances mingled with gingery aromas and the nutmeg-like scent of the rhododendrons. The many levels of beauty and awakened senses led down new paths of prayer and communication.

And I remembered that two of the rhododendron varieties are named Blue Diamond and Moonstone—both of which seemed to describe that precious, otherworldly spiritual experience.

That day is a treasured memory for me but I know, Lord, that I don't have to travel to a meditation garden in order to pray and meditate and be awakened and aware. I have been awakened to your presence in many ordinary places—from a kindergarten to a hospital room to a kitchen-table chat with a friend. I am so grateful for the treasured moments but also for your many everyday alarm clocks.

The Old/New Flower

It's one of the oldest plants on earth—possibly a survivor of the Ice Age. Yet it's one of the newer plants for home gardens since it was considered "a terrible choice" and too difficult to grow until the 1950s. It's hard to imagine a lily on ice but that's what this plant is— the lovely lily.

I don't know who figured out the Ice Age story, but I do know that lilies adorned beautiful vases found in ancient ruins on the island of Crete—and those ruins dated to the fifteenth century B.C.! Items decorated with lilies were also found in the tombs of Egyptian Pharaohs. And the columns of Solomon's temple were adorned with "lily work." Yet, with all this history behind them, lilies frustrated the efforts of gardeners for centuries. Lilies bloomed radiantly in the wild but when transplanted, they were virus-susceptible, difficult to tame, and usually died while "in captivity."

When new hybrids were finally developed, gardeners still resisted planting them because of the lily's reputation. Eventually word got around though and soon after World War II, lilies of all colors began appearing in home gardens. These were not short-lived daylilies but blossoms that lasted and could beautify any bouquet. And that's how the "lilies of the field" moved from the Ice Age to today's backyards.

Ahhh…a reputation! It's takes time to establish a good one but once you have a bad one, it's hard to erase. Lord, you must have watched a lot of "free spirits" get a bad reputation—whether it was really deserved or not—and then have a hard time getting others to change the perception of "terrible choice" or "too difficult." Help those lilies of the field, Lord, to bloom again—and help the rest of us to be slower to judge and faster to forget, so we can welcome the once-wild ones into our gardens.

The Foxy One

The foxglove has a foxy name—and also foxy ways. It's a poison plant—but it can save lives too! Extracts of European foxglove have been used for treating heart problems for centuries because it contains the poisonous compound digitalis. In early times, some people died from this poison because little was known about the proper dosage, but today digitalis plays an important part in modern medicine.

But the foxglove has another foxy way—the way it spreads its pollen. Its tubular flowers look a bit like fingers of a glove and they grow in clusters on tall spikes. The bottom of each flower tube has a projecting lower "lip" that makes a perfect landing platform for bees—and inside the tube, there's a line of spots like the landing lights on an airfield runway! When a bee lands, he follows these spots inside the tube—to the nectar. As he feasts, pollen at the top of the tube gets dusted on top of the bee's hairy back and when he backs out of the foxglove, you can actually see the pollen grains on his fur. Then the bee buzzes away—to distribute this foxy plant's pollen! What a clever—and useful—plant.

This is just one of many plants that are like a nature-made medicine cabinet, holding secrets that can cure illness and disease.

Who knew, Lord, that our gardens could be like medicine cabinets! Who knew? Others knew centuries ago but we modern ones, in our advanced wisdom, have discounted "old wives" tales of cures and healing potions. Now we are rediscovering such "secrets." Forgive us, Lord, for too often discounting the wisdom of our aging but wise friends and relatives. Some of their foxy tales might be a bit suspect—though entertaining—but the "wisdom of the ages" is more than just a saying. Experience can be the best teacher. Help us, Lord, to respect age. Remind us to listen—and to learn.

Miss Muffet, Beware

A plant named cleome (pronounced klee-O-mee) is commonly called spiderflower, so Miss Muffet might not want it in her garden—but many other gardeners do. This plant grows to an impressive height and it has a natural ability to spread so it fits well into an informal garden and makes an ideal "hedge" to hide fencing or a view you would rather not view. Its enormous cluster flowers have petals that surround long slender stamens that protrude from the center and create a spider-like effect—which is further enhanced when tiny round seedpods form on long "whiskers." The blossoms can reach six to eight inches across but are open and airy and make a graceful appearance—so there's nothing scary about this spider.

There are many species of cleomes and although the spiderflower has wilder relatives—like the Rocky Mountain bee plant and the clammyweed—the backyard variety has "royal" names like Rose Queen, Purple Queen, and Cherry Queen.

Well, Lord, isn't that the way with families? There are usually a few wilder relatives and some rather royal ones—who give all the rest something to talk about! Lord, you made such a variety of plants, birds, fish, trees, animals, spiders, and, of course, people. I guess you knew we'd all get bored if everything was just the same. Hooray for your entertaining world of alikes, yet not-alikes. That's what makes life so interesting!

Whose Nose Is Out of Joint?

The nasturtium is a pretty little flower whose name came from Latin words which mean "twisted nose." That's because this flower has a scent that is pungent—and could twist your nose! But it is so pretty with its orange, yellow, and red blossoms and shield-like leaves. And, maybe because it's pungent, its blossoms have a peppery taste so today gourmet cooks sometimes add organically grown nasturtiums to salads for a colorful, dramatic flourish.

Mine aren't organically grown so I can't use them in salads but they do remind me of a time I got my nose twisted and out of joint.

When my Great Uncle Lee died, I was twelve years old and my mother, sister, and I went to his home in Indiana to bring back a few family mementos. One was a charming old pitcher that had belonged to my great-grandmother. It was pale green with a spray of bright nasturtiums painted on it. I coveted that pitcher. I don't know why or what I would have done with it but I wanted that pitcher.

My sister was already married and had a china cabinet and that's where the pitcher went—even though she loved pink roses and her china had pink roses that did not match yellow and red nasturtiums.

Through the years, when I visited my sister for happy weekends in Tennessee, I would always take a secret peek at the pitcher. Every time I left, my sister sent me home loaded down with goodies—her homemade pickles and preserves, flower cuttings from her garden, and family pictures. At the end of one trip, she said, "I know you've always liked Uncle Lee's pitcher so I have it packed up for you to take home."

I was so excited, I didn't even have the couth to say, "Oh no, you keep it." It's been in *my* china cabinet ever since.

Now every time I look at the nasturtium pitcher, I am reminded of my great-grandmother and Great Uncle Lee. But my first and fondest thought goes to my sister—the prettiest, kindest sister, the best cook, the perfect homemaker for her extended family. And the most generous giver of gifts.

Thank you, Lord, for making sisters—and for gifting my family with the sweetest one in the world.

Purple Earrings

Evidently the fuchsia (fyoo-shuh) and I have something in common. There is a poem that is oft-quoted that suggests that when you "get old," you can do things you never did before—like wear a purple dress and a red hat. And I hear there are even clubs in various cities now where ladies "of a certain age" meet for lunch or dinner in a restaurant and they all wear purple dresses and red hats! Well, combining purple and red never stopped the fuchsia—or me.

The fuchsia wears wildly wonderful blossoms in shades of purple, white, and red. And the pendulous blossoms are sometimes called "lady's ear drops" because they look like ladies' bright dangling earrings. But those "earrings" serve a purpose—they dangle down so they can deposit pollen on the heads of hummingbirds who are hovering below to collect nectar! How about that!

Like the fuchsia, I have often worn dangling earrings and I have combined crazy colors but unfortunately most of my outfits didn't come out as successfully as the beautiful fuschias. And I have never tried to dangle an earring on a hummingbird's head.

Lord, as you know, I also belong to a ladies club that meets to eat and chat but so far, we have not felt the need to always wear purple dresses and red hats. Who knows though—that may be our next step. At the moment, all we do is stand by our bylaws: we will never hold cards in our hands and pretend to play a game; we will never discuss deeply divisive topics (only fun ones); we will not slave in the kitchen getting the food ready when it's our turn to be the hostess. Thank you, Lord, for wildly wonderful flowers like the fuchsia and wildly wonderful friends like those in my WACY club. A little purple and red and conversation and rich desserts are truly good for the soul!

The Milky Way

The milkweed doesn't sound like a garden plant but its clusters of tiny nectar-rich flowers attract bees and butterflies—and make bright long-lasting additions to cut-flower bouquets. But one of the most interesting things about this plant is the way its seeds travel.

In the fall, it has plump teardrop-shaped pods that burst open to reveal tufts of white silk and brown seeds. The wind fluffs up the silk and it rises in the winds and floats through the air like an aerial balloon with the tiny seed looking like a basket swaying in the breeze. Could the milkweed be headed for the Milky Way?

In the summertime, Native Americans once gathered the young tender shoots of the milkweed to cook and eat like asparagus. Young Indian boys would squeeze the juice from milkweed's leaves and stems into a bowl and set it by the fire overnight—and in the morning, they would have a bowl of homemade chewing gum! Indian mothers took the silk from the pods and wove it into a soft cloth, and Indian fathers used the tall, thick stems to make rope.

What a plant: chewing gum, food, silky cloth, rope, and flying seeds! But there's more! In wartime, the milkweed's silk was once used in life preservers and in airmen's coats because it would float like cork and was as warm as wool.

Well, there you have it! A "weed" that is a wonder!

Dear Lord, how often "weeds" in the garden of life blossom into blessings—a lost job results in a better one, a lost love leads to a forever one, an unexpected and unwanted relocation ends in a move to a happier new home, new city, or even new country. Help me, Lord, to look more carefully at the "weeds" in my life and show me which ones I should be trying to dig out and which ones I should be seeing as blessings. As the Serenity Prayer says: give me the wisdom to know the difference.

Creamcups and Marshmallows

Thinking about dessert again! These flowers may sound good enough to eat but they do belong in the garden. The creamcup is a member of the poppy family and in springtime grows in meadows and fields, especially along the Pacific coast. True to its name, it is a creamy yellow cup-shaped blossom and the seeds develop in poppy-like pods. Now the mallow is another story. The hibiscus in my yard is a mallow, just one of many kinds of mallows with different shaped flowers and foliage. And there *is* a marshmallow that likes to grow where it's moist and marshy. And there *is* a sweetened confection made from the root of this plant that's called a marshmallow! But don't start digging for dessert—marshmallows can also be made with sugar, egg white, gelatin, and so on, and you can get them at the nearest grocery.

Lord, I will never forget the expression I saw on a little boy's face when it was suggested he should eat his first marshmallow—a marshmallow that had been stuck on a stick, roasted over a campfire, and now looked all black and brown and strrrange. He couldn't believe someone would want him to actually try that. But when he saw others eating a marshmallow, he did try it—and, wow, did his expression change from "not me!" to "yum yum!"

Lord, it must be awful hard for little kids when everything is new and they're always being told to try it, you'll like it. But maybe it's even harder for grownups like me. I want to believe that everything's gonna be all right but I know it might not be. Forgive me, Lord, when I lose that childlike trust and let doubt sneak in. A good friend always says, "Whatever God wants." And I know I should say that too. Even when things look black and brown and strange, I know they'll get yummy again. Life may not be all creamcups and marshmallows, but oh! how sweet it is!

Obedient Dragons

Children always love the colorful snapdragon flower because you can pinch it to make it snap open its "mouth" and pretend it is roaring like a dragon. And there's another flower that has a similar name—but not the same personality. It's sometimes called the dragonhead but it must be a tame dragon because it is also known as the obedient plant!

Unlike most plants, the obedient plant bends as you bend it! If you push down most other flower stalks, they bounce right back up, but if you push the obedient plant to bend across or twist back or around—whichever way you guide it, it obediently goes. No wonder it's so popular as a good "mixer" in flower arrangements.

At a distance, the dragonhead does not look anything like the snapdragon. The snapper has jagged leaves and a blossom that is shaped a bit like a snout (so it's sometimes called a "calf's snout"). The dragonhead grows on a tall stem with several rows of small flowers growing up the spiky stem—but if you examine it closely, each of those small flowers looks like a snapdragon! So they must be relatives—maybe distant cousins.

Sorry, Lord, to admit that I am often more like the snapdragon than the obedient plant. You give me good directions and send me to go a certain way but I am determined that I should go my way. Of course, my way usually leads to a rocky road or a dead end and I finally realize your way was the best way. Thanks for being patient, Lord, and always giving me a second chance to bend back in the right direction.

The Sunbather

While many plants wilt in the midday sun, there's one that doesn't need sunglasses or lemonade in the shade. The lantana basks in the heat and sunshine. It comes from the tropics and is a member of the verbena family. In the deep South, the lantana grows wild and in Hawaii it's considered a roadside weed. But it's a treasure in backyard gardens because once it's established, it requires little water and can thrive in even poor soil.

The lantana's flowers are small but they grow in clusters, spread fast, and make a show-stopping display of white, pink, yellow, or lavender. And they are irresistible to hummingbirds and butterflies—so if you'd like some hummers or some monarchs or swallowtails to visit your garden, plant some lantanas.

Lord, seeing the lantana basking in the summer sun while those around are wilting away reminds me of that day I was basking at the swimming pool, wearing my new sunglasses. Instead of rose-colored glasses, they had yellow lenses. Remember that day, Lord? I had just had a nice dip in the pool and was drying off, relaxing and reading a book. After a few minutes, I glanced up and everyone around the pool was picking up their towels and "stuff" and leaving. I wondered why since it was such a nice sunny day—until I took off my sun-colored glasses and realized the weather had suddenly changed and the sky was dark gray, threatening to pour down at any moment. When I put my glasses back on, all looked sunny again so I stayed out a bit longer to enjoy the view while the other swimmers wondered why I was the only one not smart enough to come in out of the rain. I guess the other flowers wonder why the lantana is not smart enough to come in out of the sun! But you, above all, Lord, know that it takes all kinds to make up a funny world like ours. And ain't it fun!

Let a Smile Be Your Umbrella

If you've ever seen pictures of fancy old church pulpits, you've probably seen the kind that looked like an upside-down bell with an umbrella over it—with a man standing in the bell making a sermon. Well, that's just the way this flower looks and it's called Jack-in-the-pulpit. I don't know who Jack was but his name sure is popular—like Jack-of-all-trades, Jack-be-nimble, Jack-in-the-box—and now here he is in a pulpit!

But the interesting thing about this plant is the umbrella! Jack uses this umbrella to keep the pollen dry. Every plant has a special way to "keep its powder dry" because only when pollen is as dry as dust can insects fly away with it and spread it around. That's the reason you see some plants bow their heads in the rain.

In August, when the umbrella has turned from green to brown and withered away, some of these plants have red berries on them—and without the umbrella to hide the berries, hungry birds, mice, and squirrels can find them and have a feast.

Lord, I have a green umbrella too and a brown umbrella and a yellow umbrella with cats and dogs printed on it (to use when its raining cats and dogs) and a red one my sister gave me that has my name daintily printed all over it. Yes, I have collected too many umbrellas just like I have collected too much junk in my basement and garage. Lord, do you think I could find a Jack-of-all-trades to help me clear that out? Yes, I know. It's another one of those jobs I've just gotta do myself. And while I'm at it, Lord, help me clear out all that junk in my head so when you send me a new idea or an inspiring thought, I'll have somewhere to put it!

August

A weed is no more than a flower in disguise,
Which is seen through at once, if love give a man eyes.

JAMES LOWELL

Achoo...God Bless You

Even the best gardens sometimes have a few weeds—and one very interesting one is called the sneezeweed. It grows in wet meadows, marshes, and ditches but can sometimes be found flowering in a garden in the late summer or early fall. This sneezer can grow as tall as five feet. It has a little yellow button head with yellow flower "streamers" that look like a ballerina's skirt. So when the wind blows, you might spot a weedy ballerina dancing in your garden.

I've never been willowy enough to wear a ballet tutu, but I've sure done my share of sneezing in the garden. So a very good thing that comes to mind when I think of a sneezeweed—or a sneeze—is the Gesundheit custom. For some strange but lovely reason, wherever you are, whatever you're doing, the minute you sneeze, friends, casual acquaintances, or even total strangers will turn to you and say, "God bless you." It's become such a custom that we hardly even think about it—but we should. Let's think about what a happy happening it is to have someone, anyone, asking God to bless us. Even if that someone doesn't really mean it, maybe God hears—and does.

Do you hear, Lord? Do you bless our sneezes? If you do, that custom is almost nice enough to make up for hay fever season. But only almost, Lord, only almost!

The Begonia and the Botanist

Begonias smile happily in my garden, lulled by the buzz of bees and the summer sun, unaware of what daring deeds and dangerous risks a botanist took to get them there.

In the nineteenth century, South America became a rich source of new plants, and several varieties of begonias were discovered there by a botanist named Richard Pearce. Pearce was known to climb peaks over twelve thousand feet high—with no equipment—to get botanical specimens. He and other botanists of his day underwent amazing hardships that are almost unimaginable now. They had no climbing gear, no modern camping paraphernalia, no proper specimen containers—and they had to carry everything with them, including paper for pressing plants and ink for making notes.

One botanist had spent months collecting one hundred fifty specimens which were all lost when his boat overturned. Another carefully packed and shipped back boxes of plants which were overlooked and not opened for two years—when, of course, the plants were dead!

These men were often attacked by angry natives or, even worse, by angry mosquitoes, gnats, and fleas. Many died young from injuries, fevers, or maladies that were untreatable at the time. But they were dedicated, determined to find new plants in remote areas of the world and introduce them to the rest of the world.

Lord, thank you for all the dedicated people who have worked to give us beauty, art, cures for disease, indoor plumbing, and trips to the moon. Thank you for dedicated police and firefighters, doctors and nurses, teachers and parents. And thank you especially for those "ordinary" ones who dedicate every day to leading a good life, to being a good person, who probably never know what a great job they are doing of introducing your teachings to the rest of the world.

What Time Is It?

M y mother never seemed to have to work in her garden the way I do. She would just plant a few seeds or a cutting someone gave her and whatever it was, it grew like crazy. Every year, she would plant two or three little tomato plants and we would have so many big delicious tomatoes, she gave some away. Either it was the good Tennessee dirt or she worked in the garden when I wasn't home or the plants just liked her soft Southern drawl.

She sometimes gave things strange names, too, so I didn't really believe it when she said one of her plants was called the four o'clock. All day, this plant was just greenery until about four o'clock in the afternoon when it would suddenly burst forth with huge amounts of rosy pink tubular flowers and cover itself in glory. I always figured the four o'clock had a *real* name, but my mother just liked to call it that because of its perfect timing. Now I find out that *is* the proper name for this plant. It does have a couple of alternate names— the wishbone plant and Marvel-of-Peru—but I wouldn't have believed those names either!

Why is it, Lord, that we sometimes believe something a stranger on TV tells us but as soon as we reach the age of "reason," we become unreasonable when it comes to believing what a parent tells us. And that can even include a heavenly Father! I say "we" because I've seen it happen to others so I know I'm not the only guilty one. I guess it's all part of the process of growing and wanting to be independent—until we are "mature" and "in charge" and then wish we had someone to lean on. Actually, I did listen and believe a lot of things my mother told me and now I know I can lean on you, Lord, and I do. But I've decided, Lord, that I'm going to be more careful when I talk to my plants. Maybe they don't grow as good as my mother's did because they don't believe me!

Pop Art

A field of bright poppies in bloom is a true work of art. They are known for their rich, vivid color and their petals are as delicate as crepe paper ruffled for a party. The Oriental poppy is not easy to get started in a garden but once it makes itself at home, it pops up every year. Although one gardener called the poppy "a sly magician—one year, a brigade blooming in one corner...the next year, stragglers marching across the middle of your plot."

Through the centuries, many different types of poppies have given us beauty and have also been used in food and medicine. Early Egyptians evidently valued them because dried poppy petals have been found in Egyptian tombs dating back three thousand years. Early Greeks believed that poppy seeds made you healthy and strong, and Greek Olympic athletes often ate a mixture of poppy seeds, honey, and wine. And still today, poppy seeds make a tasty addition to breads and cakes.

Like so many plants, the poppy is more than just a pretty face.

Well, Lord, I do love poppies and poppy-seed muffins. And I know all about sly magicians—now you see 'em, now you don't. I plant something in one spot and the next year, its seeds or roots have traveled and it shows up somewhere else. It's the same with people. In today's mobile society, long-time friends are transferred away and family members get new jobs and take root in far-flung cities. And that's the good news with the bad. Missing old friends encourages us to make new ones and absence makes family reunions even fonder. But it isn't always easy to get used to so much moving and change, so help us all, Lord—to bloom where we are planted.

Smile!

The sunflower can put sunshine in the garden even on cloudy days. Like a bright cheery smile, it nods hello to all. The daisy-like blossoms are sometimes as big as a dinner plate, the stalks reaching for the house roof—but not always. The center of the sunflower is like uncut velvet and in the fall, the seeds, which are arranged a bit like a honeycomb, attract many types of songbirds. But this flower is as useful as it is cheerful. It's often grown as a money-crop since the oil from its seeds can be used in food, soap, paint, cosmetics, and so on. And its seeds can be sold for birdfeed or peoplefeed.

The sunflower is the state flower of Kansas and its pretty face can be seen on tee-shirts and every decorative item imaginable.

Of course, birds are the gardeners who plant a lot of sunflowers in backyard gardens as they fly past, dropping a seed here and there as a spring surprise for the homeowner. I've had sunflower surprises several times and it was fun to watch them grow.

Lord, wouldn't it be nice if we could all be as sunny as the sunflower? What's that you say? Okay, maybe not. If everybody was smiling all the time, we'd probably get tired of it—or get suspicious.

Just like we need sunshine and rain, I guess we need some smiling times and some not-so-smiley times. That would balance things out, right? Well, it's not working, Lord. I've had both sun and rain and my life is still unbalanced. But I do get your point. (She said with a smile!)

Catching Some ZZZs

When we first moved to the house where we live now, I found my favorite flower shop. One day I was driving along checking out the new area and went down a nearby road where there were still a few farmhouses with land around them. By the side of the road, I spotted a field full of zinnias—blooming in vivid red, yellow, orange, and all the pastels of summer. And next to the field, there was a little table with a bit of a roof over it and a few vegetables for sale. Of course, I screeched to a stop and investigated.

There was a tin can with a slot in it and instructions to weigh the vegetables you chose and leave the money in the can. That was great but the kicker was a pair of scissors next to another sign that read, "Pick your own bouquet—ten cents a flower." I had found my kind of flower shop.

For the rest of that summer and several summers after, whenever my own flowers were scarce, I would go shopping and bring home a bouquet of ZZZs. I'd arrange them in an old teapot on the kitchen table, and their pompom cheeriness would give me a smile every time I looked at them. Eventually, the little table was no longer there and the field turned into a new subdivision but sometimes now on a summer afternoon, I sit on my patio and catch another kind of ZZZs, dozing and remembering my zinnia field of dreams.

I don't think I'll ever find another flower shop I'll love as much, Lord, but I'm grateful for the summers I had that one. I'm grateful for so many other memories of simple joys, serendipities found along a country road or in the middle of a busy city. Thanks, Lord, for all the ten-cent moments that are worth a million dollars.

Mexican Hats and Hedgehogs

The prairie plant, also known as purple coneflower, is a common sight on lots of sunny prairies. And it shares a name with
a furry creature that might also visit those prairies. Although it certainly doesn't look like one, the first part of this flower's botanical
name (*Echinacea purpurea*) comes from a Greek word which means
hedgehog! That's probably because of the bristly brown seed "hat"
that sits atop its drooping daisy-like pink-purple petals. And those
petals give it another name—the nickname "droops."

To add to the excitement, there is another type of coneflower that
has a higher brown seed hat with droopy orangey petals that turn it
into a sombrero-like flower—so it's called Mexican hat plant. Ole!

But you don't have to go to a prairie to find these hardy flowers.
They are in full bloom in some of the nicest gardens I know.

*Lord, I don't think there's a hedgehog in my garden, but I'm pretty
sure there's a Mexican hat on a shelf somewhere in my basement. There's
just about everything else on a shelf in that basement but that's another story. The thing that helps me identify most with this flower is
the nickname droops. Many mornings I look in the mirror and see a
coneflower—petals drooping, hedgehog hairdo. But then, I look out
and about and feel how lucky I am to be welcoming the morning and I
raise up that hedgehog head and shout, "This is the day the Lord has
made. Let us rejoice and be glad!" And I am.*

The Dark of Night

It isn't a deep, dark secret but it *is* true that lots of plants bloom only in the dark of night. Maybe they like to be mysterious or maybe they're just shy. These plants include moonflowers, sweet-scented flowering tobacco, and evening primroses. There are even night-blooming daylilies (what a contradiction!)

There's also a night-blooming tree called the angel's trumpet tree. In the daytime, the trumpet-shaped blooms hang their heads, looking wilted, but when dusk arrives, the leaves fold down and the blossoms stand up and perfume the whole yard!

But wait—there's more! A climbing perennial cactus named Queen of the Night blooms only at night—and only once a year! If you happen to be near at just the right moment, you can watch the blossom open and fill the air with fragrance. But few people ever see the blooms fully open because they only last a few hours—and if you miss it, you have to wait another year!

One person described a garden of after-dark flowers as an enchanting oasis, a perfect place to sit and relax after the sun has set, to think about the day that has passed and drink in the beauty and the perfume of the late-bloomers.

Unlike me, these night-owl flowers are truly exotic but I can identify with them because, as you know, Lord, I too am a late-bloomer. Dawn is not my finest hour. I can pretend to be awake and be on time for early morning appointments—but just barely. My petals open slowly like that once-a-year blossom. By the end of the day, I enjoy the mystery of the nighttime garden, drinking in the evening fragrance, making a wish on the first star or the new moon. Maybe I'm just lazy, Lord, but I'm gonna have to let the early birds have the worms while I wait for the moonflowers. Thanks for the enchanting oasis of the night.

Yucky or Not?

Whenever you offer kids anything new or nutritious, some of them immediately say "Yuck!" so those kids should really like the plant named yucca. They might also be interested to know that bats like to visit this plant to get its nectar (although Batman probably does *not*), and moths get pollen from the plant and roll it into a ball under their chins. What great kid fun—bats, moths, rolling food into a ball under your chin, and a plant with a yucky name!

Actually, the yucca is definitely *not* yucky. Although it's a desert plant, it can live happily in your garden and makes a splashy appearance. It's a "rosette" of large sword-shaped leaves that reach up *and* down like a green fountain and it flowers irregularly with a spectacularly tall spike of white flowers.

But the interesting thing about this plant is that it has a "symbiotic relationship" with a moth. The yucca moth caterpillar can eat *only* yucca seeds and the yucca plant can *only* be pollinated by the yucca moth—so they need each other, help each other, and live happily ever after together.

We should all be like the yucca, Lord—needing, helping, and living happily together. And yet it doesn't always work out that way. There are people in my life that I need and who help me and I think I couldn't live without them—but even though I wouldn't want to live without them, I know I could. That's because I know that You are the only one I couldn't live without. I feel sad for those who don't have You in their lives, Lord. You and I don't have a symbiotic relationship because you sure don't need me, but I will always need you. So please stick around!

Plants to Dye For!

As soon as people figured out how to make cloth out of plants—like cotton and flax—they probably started wondering how to make that cloth into colors as bright as those of the flowers in the garden. And the experiment began. Long before modern synthetic dyes were concocted, people found ways to use plants to put more color into their lives. As you might say today—they made cloths to dye for!

A plant called woad was used as a blue dye until the seventeenth century when it was replaced by blue dye from tropical indigo plants. Weld, or dyer's rocket, was cultivated in Yorkshire, England, and other centers of the wool industry, to be used as a greenish yellow dye for coloring wool. Another (perhaps similar) plant known as dyer's greenweed was a source of yellow dye which could be turned green by mixing it with woad. Boiled madder roots made a rich, tomato red pigmentation, and safflower florets produced a range of yellow and tan dyes used in India. Even boiled red onion skins were used to dye cloth brown. And these are just a few of the many plants that, through the years, have left the garden to work in the fashion world!

My, my, aren't we the clever ones. Humans are always searching for a way to make something—and then make it better. Without the searching, we'd all still be living in caves and wearing leaves instead of fashion's latest favorite color. One of the greatest gifts you gave your people, Lord, was imagination. Thank you. Without it, we might not be as busy or as stressed as we are but life sure would be boring.

Your gift of imagination, Lord, is so great, it is to die for!

September

My good hoe as it bites the ground revenges my wrongs,

and I have less lust to bite my enemies.

In smoothing the rough hillocks,

I smoothe my temper.

RALPH WALDO EMERSON

Is There a Doctor in the House?

B ack in "olden" days, medical treatment was very limited and people often used plants and their roots to make potions to treat various illnesses. The yarrow plant was used to stop the flow of blood from a wound and so it was also called bloodwort or woundwort. As late as the American Civil War (in the 1860s), battle-field surgeons crushed yarrow plants and applied them to bullet and shrapnel wounds.

The yarrow has lacy gray-green leaves and large flat-topped flower clusters on tall sturdy stems. The blooms are usually bright yellow or white and show up vividly in the garden and also in fresh or dried flower arrangements. The yarrow came to America with early set-tlers and was used in many ways—to make an astringent lotion, to treat a cold, to brew beer, and to stir up healing concoctions. One "recipe" called for a mixture of yarrow, brandy, and gunpowder. It was prescribed to ease pain—and I bet it did!

We have much better potions and finer hospitals today, Lord, but sometimes they don't heal or cure any better than the earlier ones that we might laugh about. We've come to expect miracles from modern medical technology—and from you, Lord—but sometimes we don't get the result we want from either one. It's very hard to face loss when we pray so hard for healing and the answer is no. Help us to accept your will, Lord. Thank you for all the modern medicines that do cure and heal. And thank you for all the prayers that are answered yes.

What's in a Name?

The name of one plant tells it all—it's called the butterfly bush. Its branch ends produce long clusters of fragrant flowers that are evidently a butterfly's dream come true. The flowers resemble lilacs, and the blooms of white, pink, red, or lilac make a pretty picture in the garden. But the picture gets even better when the blooms are visited by hummingbirds, songbirds, and, of course, butterflies.

This bush is at its best in late summer when its flower perfume attracts many different, colorful types of its namesake. As butterflies bury their heads in the blossoms, busily drinking nectar with their wings aflutter, it looks like the butterfly bush is actually abloom with butterflies!

This plant was discovered in China and sent to Kew Gardens in England by Dr. Augustine Henry, an Irish customs officer in Shanghai and assistant medical officer at Ichang. He was a man ahead of his time, concerned about air purity and deforestation, as well as plants and flowers. And today his butterfly bush has flown from Shanghai to England to many gardens—including mine.

Thank you, Lord, for sending butterflies to decorate our gardens. Sometimes on days when I feel "bushed," I like to pretend that I am a social butterfly and I dress up in what I hope will look appropriate and go to a "veddy" fancy shopping mall. The only kind of shopping I can afford to do there is window shopping but I flutter from window to window, watching what the other butterflies are wearing and pretending that I have just flown by on my way to tea at the Ritz. Having had my taste of nectar, I come home, have a cup of tea in my cozy kitchen and look out the window at my garden in bloom and the butterfly bush—and I feel richly blessed. Thanks, Lord, for making all kinds of butterflies—even the pretend ones like me.

 SEPTEMBER

Mum's the Word

The name chrysanthemum comes from the Greek words for "gold" and "flower," and it certainly is a golden autumn flower although it also has other colors today. It also has other names—such as mum, feverfew, and even "God's eyebrow."

In China, where it bloomed for over twenty-five hundred years before it came to the West, the chrysanthemum was known as one of the four "noble" plants. The other three were bamboo, plum, and orchid. Those three aren't too popular in home gardens today, but at least we can be proud that we have one noble one!

Shapes of this flower range from the button mum—which resembles a button—to the bit larger cushion mum to the pompom mum which was first grown in France and got its name because it looked like the pompoms on sailor's hats.

The pompom mum has been one of the "terrible" disappointments of my life. When I was a kid, we lived several blocks from a college football stadium and the university's colors were gold and black. At that time, it was the custom for guys to give their dates a florist's corsage of one huge yellow pompom tied with ribbon streamers of gold and black. On Saturday afternoons, I would watch as cars parked all along our street and young ladies got out of the cars looking beautiful with their pompoms. I coveted those corsages. By the time I was old enough to get a date to go to those football games, either the custom had changed or my date didn't believe in pompoms. I never got one.

You see what a terribly disadvantaged youth I had, Lord? Oh well, I've had lots of other kinds of cushions in my life so I guess I shouldn't complain. Mum's the word.

Psst!...Pass It On...

When there's a bit of news or a juicy rumor, it passes along from ear to ear until it spreads all over town—and that's the same thing that happens with "passalong plants." You visit a friend's garden and admire a plant and soon you're going home with a cutting to plant in *your* garden. Then someone comes to visit you and goes home with a sprig of mint, a clump of daylilies or whatever they admire or whatever you feel like sharing.

In my first garden, I carefully planted honeysuckle and mint from my mother's yard. One morning I discovered a rabbit had eaten all the leaves from my mint and I was heartbroken. I had no idea that mint is indestructible and would soon return and take over that side of the yard. The honeysuckle also found a home and grew all over my back fence, and I loved the blossoms and the sweet aroma— but soon some poison ivy from the farm behind us made friends with the honeysuckle and it turned into a mixed blessing!

When we moved to our current home, I brought along some double daylilies that had first bloomed in Aunt Linnie's garden and were passed along to my mother's garden, then my sister's, and then mine. Every time they burst into bloom, it's a family reunion!

I also have a lilac bush grown from a tiny twig from a stranger's garden, a fringe tree from my sister, and a different kind of mint which I brought home the day I came out of a restaurant and spotted a pile of mint the gardener had thinned out and was getting ready to throw away. Ah, yes, I do love those passalong plants.

Lord, I also love my little prayer group of friends who meet each week and pass along family happenings, funny stories, information from books they've read, ideas from sermons they've heard, sad news and good news and many troubles or intentions that need to be prayed about. Thank you, Lord, for passalong plants and passalong friends.

The Garden Wall

Who wants to be a wallflower? The wallflower does! Given this name because it was first grown on walls, it has several species. One is described as richly fragrant with a rainbow of colors, perfect for rock gardens or filling in gaps of stone walls, a must for informal borders or cottage gardens. Another is described as having a sweet, spicy fragrance as charming as its golden orange blossoms. Other varieties are described as having large clumps of pink flowers or magenta flowers or salmon flowers. This wallflower really gets around.

Who knows who first used the term wallflower to describe the poor unfortunate one who stands by the wall, waiting to be asked to dance or hoping to get chosen for the team. Maybe the term was never meant to have that meaning at all. Maybe it was first used as a compliment for a very beautiful lady, like the flower, fragrantly blossoming by the wall!

Lord, Lord, how often I open mouth and insert foot so that words come out in a way I never meant. I say something, intending to be complimentary, and instead the words that come out sound insulting. The person I was "complimenting" looks at me in shocked silence and the more I try to remove the foot, the further it gets stuck in. I know how it feels to be a wallflower and I wouldn't want anyone to feel that way because of something I said. So, please, Lord, the next time I try to think of a compliment, remind me not to say something like, "You are as fragrant as a wallflower."

The Dinosaur's Garden

One garden resident has been around so long it's called a prehistoric plant and is thought to have grown on earth as far back as the age of the dinosaurs. Its family is widely varied—with members large and small who can live in dry or wet lands, with sun or shade. Yes, it's the ancient fern family. Maybe you have some in your garden or in your house. You can choose from maidenhair, ostrich, cinnamon, rabbit's foot, five-finger fern—and many more. Wherever they grow, ferns provide a lovely oasis of greenery.

And there's a wonderful fern fairy tale. In olden times, ferns were thought to be magical plants and it was said that if you sprinkled fern dust in your shoes, you could become invisible!

But where could you get this magic fern dust? It's easy! Just look under the frond of a fern and you will probably see some little brown dots. Take a piece of white paper and lay the frond on the paper with the brown dots facing down and leave it overnight (for the fairies to come???). The next morning, you will see a dusting of fine brown powder. You might have to use a lot of fronds if you have big shoes to fill. You'll have to use a lot of imagination too. I tried it and I'm sure I was invisible but no one seemed to notice.

Dear Lord, you must have used a lot of fern dust, because so far you are the only one who has managed to be invisible! I wish you would clean out your shoes so we could all see what you look like but I guess you know best. Since we can't see you, we can each imagine that you look just the way we want you to look. And maybe if I could see you, I would be so awed, I'd be afraid to talk to you the way I do now. So keep the fern dust in your shoes, and I will keep watering the pretty fern in my living room and the wandering fern on the front porch and I will keep filling your ears with my tales of woe and wonder.

Honestly Now!

Most people are not happy to think they or anything they own is "going to seed," but there's a plant that is at its best when it's gone to seed! That is the honesty plant, but we always called it the money plant or the silver-dollar plant.

The honesty starts as a quiet little green plant with small purple flowers, but then it magically produces silvery seedpods that look like silver dollars!

Even the seedpods start out quietly. Each oval has three layers and the two outer layers are paper-thin and colorless but when you rub your fingers across the ovals, the two paper-thin outer layers come off, black seeds fall out and you're left with a shimmery silvery bouquet that looks like a work of art and is now in great demand for dried flower arrangements. In fact, florists sell the pretty sprays of silver-dollar plants for a pretty price!

To be honest, when I was a kid, we used to play with the silver dollars and give them no respect. Now that honesty is expensive, I keep getting seeds from friends and trying to grow my own money plant but I'm sorry to report, there is no honesty in my garden today.

No money and no honesty, Lord—sounds a lot like our beleaguered government. Well, I shouldn't say that. There are a lot of good politicians and we have many reasons to be proud of our government. But the honest politicians don't seem to be able to grow a money plant as fast as the not-so-honest ones. Now look who's talking! I can't grow money either although I've sure tried—honestly! Guess I should do more praying and less criticizing. So, Lord, please bless—and advise— our politicians so they will be more honest and spend less of our silver dollars. And please help me to do the same thing!

The Wedding Gift

Once upon a time, in the kingdom of Denmark, a royal prince planned a romantic wedding gift for his bride. It was in the eighteenth century, a time when there was great interest in botanical study and the classification of plants. Now a few years before the wedding, Denmark had produced a glorious, illustrated florilegium (anthology) of its native plants—showing roots, bulbs, leaves, and Latin names. It was titled *Flora Danica* or Plants of Denmark. According to the story, Crown Prince Frederick decided to have his royal manufactory produce a set of the finest gilded, hand-painted porcelain—with each piece depicting a different plant from the Flora Danica! This unique gift must surely have delighted his bride, Catherine II, Czarina of Russia.

Unfortunately, the *complete* set of one thousand eight hundred and two pieces was not ready by the wedding day. Even more unfortunately, by the time the painstaking masterwork was finished twelve years later, the Czarina had died!

However, the royal china lived happily ever after—to be cherished by, and to inspire, the nation that created it. This amazingly beautiful china depicts three thousand flowers, mosses, and mushrooms of Denmark plus plants from Greenland, Iceland, and the Faeroe Islands, which were all owned by Denmark at that time. And the work continues. Today, highly trained artists of Royal Copenhagen still paint perfect flowers freehand, with copper plate engravings of the original Flora Danica as their guide. Today collectors can choose new sets or seek out old pieces at estate sales, auctions, and so on. The prince's royal gift lives on.

Of course, Lord, I know a family can have a feast using grocery-store china and jelly glasses for goblets—as long as they gather together. But it's wonderful to see your plants celebrated in such a royal way. And it's a reminder to us to make and keep family traditions, to take pride in workmanship, to appreciate the uniqueness of our native country, to treasure our family trees, and to give thanks for the florilegium of our many blessings!

Fashionably Late Flowers

Good things come to those who wait—and that's true in the autumn garden. After the early arrivals of spring and the colorful crowds of summer, there's still more to welcome—the "fashionably late" comers to the party.

Those include the red-hot poker plant, or torch lily, which brings a splash of color with its two-tone red and yellow flower spikes and the prairie sage which waits until early fall to send up its own bright spikes of azure blue. Then there's the light purple flowers of Joe-Pye-weed (which was named after a colonial era medicine man) and the mistflower's clusters of blue-purple flowers.

Mingle that bunch with some fountain grass and you have quite a fall festival. The fountain grass has bright green foliage in spring but in the fall, it turns into a rich golden brown and has bottle-brush flower heads which ripen to a contrasting red-brown. As the tall grass moves in a last summer dance, its autumn outfit blending with the other bright colors, you could almost imagine the latecomers celebrating with a fireworks display!

Always love fireworks, Lord. Always hate it when the last bright spark fades. Always hate it when anything bright and beautiful goes away. Autumn is a time of change, Lord, a time of remembering bright and beautiful sparks that are no more—and change is hard. But when it's time for the summer sparklers to leave, you give us the gold, crimson, and burnt orange of tree leaves plus those late flower fireworks to ease the farewells. Thank you, Lord, for all the ease-ments you send to spark the fire of acceptance every time we have to say good-bye.

October

Nobody sees a flower, really—it is so small—
we haven't time, and yet to see takes time,
like to have friends takes time.

GEORGIA O'KEEFE

It's a Flact!

Ever since ancient times, one plant has made an important contribution to society. It's the flax plant—and that's a flact!

The oldest textile fabric known is linen which is made from flax. And then there's linseed oil which is made by pressing flax seeds and is used to make paints And, on top of all that, this plant has graceful gray-green stems and periwinkle blue flowers that open in the morning and close up to take a nap at noon so it also makes a pleasant contribution to gardens.

Turning a plant into a pretty linen dress takes a bit of doing. The flax stems are soaked to soften them and then beaten to break the stems into fibers that resemble very dry blond hair. Next the fibers are combed and carded, spun into threads and woven into fabric—and made into many useful things.

Flaxen linen is even mentioned in the Bible and was used at that time for clothing, sails for ships, curtains, and even burial shrouds. You've probably heard of the most famous shroud of all—the Shroud of Turin—which some people believe is the shroud in which Jesus was buried. The Shroud of Turin is made of linen.

Who could imagine that such a small quiet plant could make such a large contribution to the world around it? Who could believe that a small quiet person could make a large contribution by working for years to make a wonderful new scientific discovery or maybe just by spending years working and praying for others? Well, of course, you could imagine that, Lord, since you made both plants and people. You sure did a good job. Thanks.

Anyone for Tea?

There's a great legend that says tea drinking was invented by the Chinese Emperor Shen Nung in 2737 B.C. when some leaves from burning tea twigs flew into a pot of water he was boiling. A few thousand years later, in 1650, tea was brought from China to Europe and now the British brew about 180,000 tons of tea leaves every year! And not to be outdone, Americans now brew about 31,000 metric tons of tea each year! I brew a few of those leaves myself and maybe you do too.

You probably *don't* have a tea plant in your garden but if you did, it would have pretty white blossoms on it. And you could plant some of the herbs used to make tea. The aromatic herb camomile has daisy-like flowers that can be steeped to make a soothing tea that is supposed to be good for restless children or a cure for nightmares. Dried leaves from the herb bergamot give the well-known Earl Grey tea its distinctive taste. And wandering mint makes tea too!

A few years ago when we went to England, we drank lots of tea. And, in our hotel room, there was a tea set with everything you needed to prepare afternoon tea. I fell in love with the charming china tea caddy that was painted with flowers and their botanical names. When I asked the hotel if I could possibly buy the caddy, they wrapped it carefully and I brought it home as my favorite souvenir. Every time I look at it, I am reminded of the lush flowers blooming in every nook and cranny of England.

Thank you, Lord, for all the different countries and customs and for today's opportunities to travel and see how the rest of the world lives. It's wonderful to wander but it's always best to come home again. Bless all your children, Lord, who may have wandered from your garden paths. Help them find the right answers to their questions, and lead them safely home again.

Getting Squashed!

Yes, yes, I know pumpkins and squash are not flowers but their vines *do* have pretty yellow flowers in early summer and by October, it's pumpkin patch and jack-o'-lantern time. Pumpkin vines do like to spread around so other plants can get "squashed" by them but if there's lots of room in your backyard, you can grow a nice-sized pumpkin in time for Halloween. And there are pretty varieties of squash and gourds that make nice table arrangements when there are few flowers left in the garden.

Pumpkins have provided food—and fun—in our part of the world for thousands of years. And, although native to Africa, gourds dating from 7000 B.C. have been found in South America. It is thought they may have drifted there from Africa on ocean currents because experiments have shown that seeds can remain viable inside gourds that have floated in sea water for two hundred twenty days! Tales of floating gourds, carved pumpkins, and that never-ending zucchini bread—what a fall festival!

Lord, I have always been too smart to plant zucchini in my yard but my neighbors did and were oh-too-happy to share. I did grow a nice pumpkin once and that was great fun. And I love to decorate the house and dress up and have Halloween parties. I used to make stew and cook it inside a hollowed-out pumpkin and serve it from the pumpkin for Halloween but nobody else got as excited about it as I did. But that's okay. I get excited about a lot of things that nobody but you and I seem to celebrate. Thanks for being my secret pal of celebrations, Lord. We make a great team.

A Gawky Yard Bird

The Flamingo nandina sometimes sports gawky, leggy stalks and awkward plumes of foliage and gives a good plant a bad name. But it's the gardener's fault, not the nandina's. This plant needs pruning! And just plain pruning won't do. If you start lopping and chopping, without a plan, the nandina will look like a gawky kid with a bad haircut. But if you prune correctly, you'll have a shrub with layers of lacy leaves year-round that really shows off in cold weather. That's when the leaves blush with a reddish tinge and the branches are filled with spectacular clusters of cheery bright berries that look like little bunches of red grapes.

Mockingbirds, cedar waxwings, and robins will decorate your yard as they feast on these berries and, if there are any berry clusters left, you can harvest them to use in wreaths or mantle arrangements. But don't forget that winter is just the time for "stairstep" pruning. First, you look through the bush and cut one-fourth of the stems down to the ground. Next, you cut one-fourth of random stems to one-third the height of the plant. Then you cut another one-fourth of random stems to two-thirds the height of the nandina. And then you leave the rest of the stems uncut. This tough, old-fashioned ever-green plant makes a nice screen and a good backdrop for other plants—*if* it gets that proper pruning.

I pity the poor nandina, Lord, getting blamed for being shaggy when all it needs is a good haircut. I know just how that feels. A bad haircut can turn even a tough, old-fashioned person into a gawky hide-the-head who wants to stand in the corner so no one will notice. Yes, Lord, I know there are a lot worse problems and I never pray to ask for a good haircut (although I really want to). At least in the winter, I can wear a hat to cover a bad "do" but the nandina can't. So, Lord, bless the nandina—and bless all of us who occasionally need a bit of pruning!

Sooo Soft

Many plants have been used for medicines or healing balms but there's one that was once even used for bandages! It's the oh-so-soft lamb's ears. The leaves grow in lush clumps and are so velvety and soft, they were often used as bandages in colonial days. The person who named it must have thought the grayish leaves were not only the same size and shape as a lamb's ears—but they also felt furry like the lamb's wool. Children—and adults—like to rub their fingers over the plant's fuzzy leaves. It's the kind of plant you love to touch!

And when slender stems with loose spikes of pinkish flowers rise from the clump of leaves, some gardeners think the flowers are unattractive and remove them so they won't detract from the beauty of the leaves. This is quite the reverse of most plants since the leaves are usually just a background for the flowers.

Well, Lord, it seems every leaf has its day! Guess you made lots of flowers and then felt bad because the leaves were being overlooked so you decided to make some plants where the leaves were the stars. You're very good at that, Lord. You make some quiet, un-noticeable kids who seem to fade into the background, gentle as a lamb, while others take center stage. But often it's the quiet lambs that grow up to lead worthwhile lives of service to others. Thank you, Lord, for all kinds of plants and kids, and teach us all to value the background leaves as well as the blossoms.

A Windy Story

Once upon a time, many years ago, Native Americans often camped near a big lake where one of their favorite plants flowered and grew and filled the air with an oniony odor. They liked to use this plant—either fresh picked or dried—in cooking. Today we call it the wild leek, but because of its odor, they called it skunk plant. And, since it grew so freely there, they called the area by the lake the "Shi-ka-ko," or place of the skunk. And so—you guessed it—when a big city grew up there, it was named Chicago!

Well, I don't know if that's a true story but it is a fun one. The Indians' sikakushia is similar to the garlic grown today for cooking. It's a cousin to the onion grass that sprouts in lawns and gives a springtime smell to fresh-cut yards. It's also a cousin to the daffodil, tulip, lily, and hyacinth since they all grow from bulbs beneath the ground where they store their food.

But the sikakushia has *two* bulbs—one under and one above ground! Its tall stalk grows from a bulb and then is topped with a little cluster of pointed bulbs. From this "outside" bulb, long thin green whiskers shoot out and then the whiskers blossom with little pink flowers. So this is a very interesting looking plant—whether it grows in the Windy City or in your backyard!

Lord, I hope others enjoy these long-winded stories as much as I do. You must have put all these "storied" plants on earth so we'd have something to talk about. You put lots of long-winded stories in the Bible, too, so we'd have something to read about. Thanks for entertaining us so well, Lord. We needed that.

Boo! It's a Ghost!

When you're hiking or taking an autumn walk in this month of Halloween, you just might come upon a spooky vision in the dark woods—a group of white stalks sprouting from a bed of dead leaves.

And on the top of each stalk, you'll see a ghostly white flower with its head bowed. Without a shred of green and needing no sunlight to bloom, these are called ghost flowers.

You won't be growing these in your garden because they only live in the woods, taking nourishment, as mushrooms do, from decaying plants or leaves. However, they are *not* mushrooms but a member of the wintergreen family. And they are sometimes called Indian-pipes.

The flowers are pure white when they first sprout. As they age, the bowed head rises and then they slowly turn to pink and then to lilac and finally to black—as though to mourn their fading life. But they drop seeds and come back again the next year.

Lord, you certainly have planted some strange things on this planet for us to discover. Naturalists are delighted when they come across these unusual plants, saying that they are indeed strange but very beautiful. Perhaps the ghost flowers are a reminder to us that a plant can be beautiful even if it doesn't fit our preprogrammed idea of how a plant should look—just like some people can be beautiful even if they don't fit our preprogrammed idea of how they should look or act or feel or dress. Lord, I know you gave us free will but I wonder who did all that preprogramming. Hmmm....

The Friendly Witch

When I was a little girl and would get a scrape or scratch, my mother would often "treat" it by sloshing on a soothing but astringent potion called witch hazel. Since I was snuffling with my big bad boo-boo, I didn't like the idea of being treated with something that included the word *witch*. However, I was intrigued about the Hazel part—since both my mother and sister included Hazel in their names!

The two of them were two of the sweetest people on earth so I was consoled, thinking Hazel must be a friendly witch. Since then, I have discovered that witch hazel is a lotion made from the bark of a small tree or shrub by the same name. The native witch hazel blooms in the late fall but there are several varieties, and one or the other is in bloom from October to April.

The very fragrant blossoms are unique ribbonlike flowers that bloom on bare branches and will unfurl on sunny days even if there is snow on the branches. These shrubs can grow from six to twelve feet tall—which is much taller than my little mother ever grew. She *was* like them though because she could bloom in the snow. She once dyed mashed potatoes pink and pushed them through a pastry tube to serve us a platter of pink roses in winter. She would turn out feasts for every holiday even though she had a tiny apartment-sized stove. And she helped me learn to find fun in every day.

Lord, you really did a great job when you created the witch hazel and my mother Hazel and my sister Hazelmai. Thanks.

November & December

The Lord will guide you always,
He will satisfy your soul in drought,
You shall be like a watered garden.

ISAIAH 53:11

The Ivy League

As the holiday season approaches, all is brown and quiet in my yard—except the ivy that stays green and hardy all year in front of my front porch. When you think of ivy, you often envision ivy-covered buildings on a revered college campus or lush ivy borders at a botanical garden. Yet this is also a down-home plant that grows in many gardens and around many humble abodes. You might say it's a plant combination of Cary Grant and Uncle Jethro.

Now everyone says ivy is easy to grow but in my yard, ivy is easy to grow only where it wants to grow. I delight in the porch border, but I want it to continue down each side of our long front walk. Since it never wandered there on its own, I took cuttings and rooted and planted it there. It died. I bought ivy from a nursery and planted it there. It died. Ignoring my pleas, it went in the other direction and grew under my bushes where only the neighborhood cat enjoys it when he hides under there for his afternoon nap.

I like the cat and I like the ivy but obviously I have no control over either one. Maybe it's because they are both down-home *and* sophisticated and they know I am only down-home. Oh well, I will gather bunches of ivy to add sophistication to my Christmas bouquets and all my down-home friends will love it.

Thanks, Lord, for the lush green-all-year ivy that brightens my yard. Thanks, too, for all the different kinds of people you send my way to brighten my days—both the elegant ones and the comfortable ones. Variety is what makes the bouquet of life so interesting.

The December Decorator

Some folks say their favorite Christmas plant is one that decorates itself for the holidays—the Christmas cactus. These plants last for years and sometimes for generations! And they decorate themselves with bright red blooms just in time to say Merry Christmas. One lady said her cactus has been passed along in the family and is now more than one hundred years old. Another said that last December her cactus had over five hundred blooms on it. Another says hers is easy to live with because it seems to thrive on neglect!

Although most cactuses or cacti are sticky sorts with needles ready to prick you, it seems the Christmas cactus can be a welcome member of the family. And it also makes an easy Christmas gift. Although I haven't tried it, they say you can just take a cutting of a new shoot, stick it in some good potting soil and it will start to grow almost immediately. All you have to do is provide a pretty pot and you have a great gift that might last for years to come.

What more could anyone ask—a Christmas bloomer, easy to grow, long-lasting, makes its own decorations, and provides inexpensive gifts for friends! Actually, Lord, I know some people like this plant. They're easy to get along with, are always giving little gifts to others, are blooming with good cheer, and will be your friend forever. They're great role models and I thank you, Lord, for putting them in my life. With friends like that, who needs any other kind of gifts for Christmas!

Deck the Halls

I've never decked my halls with boughs of holly because I love to see those cheery red berries and pointy green leaves every time I look out my window. Someone planted them in my yard before I moved here and it's taken them a long time to grow. I only allow myself to cut just a few small branches—but never boughs—to add to Christmas arrangements.

One of my hollies is tall and mighty and the other is tall and skinny—and when the snows come, the skinny one gets so weighted down, it bends lower and lower until I'm afraid it will break. That's when I grab my boots and my broom and dash out to sweep and shake and try to ease the burden so my friend can stand tall again. Of course, there are all kinds of holly—including American holly, Japanese holly, coral holly, inkberry, Old Heavy Berry, and sparkle-berry—and they add a happy touch to Christmas around the world.

Sometimes I feel just like my skinny holly, Lord—weighted down with all the Christmas chores and bending lower and lower every day. But then I remember the year I helped the first-graders put on a Christmas pageant and we made costumes with crayons and paper bags and Mary had a veil of white tissue paper, and it was truly a holy night. With that picture in my head, I forget the chores and remember the joy and become Sparkleberry—until I eat Christmas dinner and then I turn into happy Old Heavy Berry. Fa-la-la-la-lah!

Gold and What?

Even children know that gold is always a good gift, but they often wonder why "wise" men would bring something strange like frankincense and myrrh to a baby. Why not some really good toys, a teddy bear, or even a car seat?

In biblical times, those two gifts were probably even more precious than gold. It was a time when there was a lot of disease and very little medical knowledge so people used strange "cures." Frankincense is an aromatic gum resin that you get by making incisions in the trunk of a special tree. This resin was burned to try to "purify" the air with its smoke whenever there was someone in the house with a serious disease. It was also used as a tonic, a sleeping potion and for many medical "treatments."

Myrrh comes from a different tree—a small thorny one—and its name comes from an Arabic word which means "bitter" because it has a pungent taste. It was commonly used as a mouthwash for mouth and throat problems and even as an eyewash. Like frankincense, it was considered a cure-all for a long list of problems—arthritis, indigestion, typhoid, and so on. And it was prescribed for the postnatal care of both mother and child. For people who had very little medical care, cure-alls could be even more valuable than gold.

In our more fortunate times, frankincense, myrrh, and gold have become Christmas symbols. As a remembrance of the wise men, you might order the two "strange" gifts from an herb shop and use small bags of frankincense and myrrh plus a small bouquet of dried marigolds as stocking stuffers or package tie-ons.

Lord, so many things have changed and so many things remain the same. Christmas today has become a shopping, cooking, baking "marathon" instead of a spiritual time of prayer and thanksgiving. Yet the glory and the joy and the awesomeness of it all is still there, under the wrapping paper and the hurried preparations. Somehow, the star still shines, the miracle still fills us with wonder and your amazing "gift" still surprises us with its generosity and love. All praise and glory be thine! And happy birthday.

Star Light, Star Bright

There's a plant that does *not* bloom in December, but it should because it's called the Star of Bethlehem. It has small star-shaped greenish-white blossoms that bloom in a cone-shaped cluster atop a slender stem above shimmering ribbon-like leaves. It is nicely fragrant and it's easy to see how it got that name.

There's another plant that does *not* bloom in December, but it should because it's named Christmas bells. It has chubby little lantern-shaped flowers that dangle from slim stems. The blossoms are a golden orange and the soft green narrow leaves sometimes taper into threadlike tendrils. I don't know why it isn't called Christmas lanterns, but it isn't.

And, yes, there's still another plant that does *not* bloom in December but should because it's the Christmas rose. It has cup-shaped flowers in pale tints like white or pink—with freckles of a deeper pink or red near the center.

The star and the bells bloom in spring or summer and the rose shows up in late winter or early spring. Who knows where they got those names but why not! It's nice to have Christmas in March or Christmas in June—so we can remember the Christmas spirit even long after it's over.

Now wouldn't that be lovely, Lord, if we could keep the Christmas spirit all year 'round—decorate the house, sing songs, get together with family and friends, and be of good cheer. Well, some families really do do those things all year 'round—and aren't they the lucky ones. No, I guess they are the blessed ones. Thank you, Lord, for flowers that take the name of Christmas into the spring and summer and thank you for all the good folks who "keep" Christmas all year 'round.

The Ambassador

Probably the most popular December flower is the poinsettia, which was named for Dr. J. R. Poinsett, who was the United States Ambassador to the newly independent Republic of Mexico from 1825–1829. Dr. Poinsett sent this bright flower to the U.S. so you might say the ambassador from the United States to Mexico sent the poinsettia as an ambassador from Mexico to the United States!

In Mexico, this plant became known as the Nativity Flower because it was used to decorate churches at Christmastime. In its native tropical climate, the poinsettia can be a garden flower and grow into a shrub as tall as sixteen feet high, but in the U.S. smaller plants are grown in greenhouses to be used as church *and* home decorations.

At Christmas, those big red showy flowers are everywhere—but wait! Poinsettia "flowers" aren't red! They're the tiny little yellow or greenish red "blooms" in the center of those brilliant red "bracts" or leaves that we think of as the Christmas flower!

Well, Lord, everything isn't always as it seems but it seems that the poinsettia "bracts" were a great Christmas gift from Dr. Poinsett.

Last year, someone gifted me with a cinnamon-scented hot pad that has the picture of a little bird sitting on a spray of poinsettias, with the words: "I heard a bird sing in the dark of December…a magical thing and sweet to remember."

Birdsong on a dark day, bright poinsettias on a snowy day. So many sweet things to remember. Thank you, Lord, for your wondrous "coming" at Christmas.

✄ One Last "Prayer" ✄

P lease note that I am not a horticulturist, a botanist, a florist, or
in any way qualified as an expert or professional in the care and
feeding of flowers. I hope you have enjoyed wandering through the
garden with me but please remember that I am just a backyard
gardener, a patio planter, a digger of dirt. So if I have made any
glaring mistakes in this floral fantasy, I fall to my knees and beg
your pardon.

> *As I said at the beginning of this book, gardens have often*
> *brought me to my knees—in more ways than one.*

Bernadette McCarver Snyder

Appendix

Garden Tips and Quips

This is a small bouquet
I have gathered for your pleasure:
may you meander happily!

 **APPENDIX**

In January...

- Redecorate discarded Christmas tree branches by stringing them with garlands of popcorn, cranberries, fruit, and so on, or roll pine cones in peanut butter and birdseed—to make a cafeteria for the birds.
- Use sand or birdseed for traction on icy paths so salt or ice-melters won't damage your yard.
- Gently brush heavy snow from shrub or tree branches to ease their burden.

> *He who plants a seed beneath the sod,*
> *and waits to see, believes in God.*

In February...

- Swap seeds and plant information with fellow gardeners.
- Sort through pots to get ready for spring.
- Scrub heavily encrusted clay pots with a steel-wool pad after soaking the clay pots overnight in one gallon of water and one cup each of white vinegar and bleach.
- Keep foot traffic on your lawn to a minimum when soil is wet or frozen.

> *From one small seed of kindness,*
> *friendship grows.*

In March

- Start seeds to replant later in the garden.
- Put out birdhouses and fill birdbaths.
- Avoid mulching too early in spring. The mulch may insulate the soil and keep it from warming up.
- To improve drainage in clay soil, add peat moss, leaves, compost or other organic matter.

> **Gardens are not made by
> sitting in the shade.**

In April...

- Beware of lush blooming annuals at garden centers or roadside stands. They may have been forced into early bloom and will not transplant happily until the ground is warm enough to welcome them.
- Plant markers can be made from ice-cream sticks or plastic spoons labeled with permanent ink.
- For fragrant flowers, search for old varieties instead of "designer" hybrids.

> **A flower garden in bloom
> is a backyard rainbow.**

In May...

- Only garden on days that end in Y!
- For the strongest flavor, harvest herbs just before they flower.
- Loam is the ideal soil. It contains equal parts of sand, silt, and clay.
- To encourage young gardeners, help them plant easy-to-grow flowers like petunias, marigolds, and sunflowers.

> *You'll never have to wait for someone to bring you flowers if you plant your own garden.*

In June...

- A "soaker" hose can attract hummingbirds because they like taking a bath in the fine mist it shoots out.
- Groups of containers can create charming spots of "movable" color and large planters can showcase a wonderful mix of colorful annuals in a small space.
- Container gardens dry out quickly so you may need to water every day. Clay containers and hanging baskets dry out very quickly so in very hot weather, you may need to water twice a day.
- If a pot dries out completely, set it in a large container of water for an hour or two, then move it to a shady spot until the plants perk up, then return it to its original spot.

> *One of the worst mistakes you can make when gardening is to think you are in charge.*

In July…

- Enjoy the garden on the sow-as-you-grow plan.
- Prop up branches of fruit trees when they become heavy with fruit.
- Bees collect nectar from approximately two thousand flowers to make one tablespoon of honey. And you thought gardening was hard work!
- Whenever possible, avoid overhead watering. It wastes water and can encourage the spreading of plant diseases.

> *People are like gardens—*
> *they blossom when loved.*

In August…

- Beware of fall webworms and watch for spider-mite activity.
- Plant or transplant evergreens and order fall bulbs.
- During a typical growing season, a medium-sized oak tree can give off twenty-eight thousand gallons of moisture…and a gardener can give off twenty-eight thousand moans and groans.

> *Gardening is healthy exercise if you can*
> *straighten up when you finish!*

In September...

- Harvest the last of fresh garden vegetables from those roadside stands.
- Deadhead flowers and replace any "goners" by moving around your garden pots to fill in the empty spots so the garden beauty will last a little longer.
- When the weather cools, start planting bulbs for spring bloom.

> **A garden is a thing of beauty
> and a job forever!**

In October...

- If you have sweet potatoes, pumpkins, or squash in the garden, remember to harvest them before frost. (Did you know a pumpkin root system can reach more than fifteen miles!?)
- Continue mowing the lawn until growth stops. (Even if you don't feel like it!)
- Finish planting spring bulbs—possibly among the hostas, daylilies, ground cover.
- Before planting container-grown trees and shrubs, loosen soil in the area five times the diameter of the root ball. Mulch well after watering.

> **The more one gardens,
> the more one grows.**

In November...

- Mulch flower and bulb beds after ground freezes.
- Apply diluted whitewash (equal parts of water and interior white latex paint) to southwest side of young fruit trees to prevent winter sun-scald injury.
- Cut back mums to within several inches of the ground. After ground freezes, apply a 2–3 inch layer of loose mulch.
- Shut off and drain any outdoor water pipes or irrigation systems. Store garden hoses for winter.

> **What sunshine is to flowers, smiles are to friends—or to those you encounter each day, especially in the sometimes sunless winter!**

In December...

- Water houseplants with tepid water and, on cold nights, move them away from icy windows.
- Repot root-bound houseplants.
- Clean and oil garden hand tools before storing them away for the winter.
- If you have Christmas poinsettias, they like sun for at least half a day. Keep them away from drafts and heat registers. Punch holes in foil wraps so they can drain and let soil dry only slightly between waterings.

> **The Amen! of nature is always a flower.**
> OLIVER WENDELL HOLMES